The Echo of Silence

Seyed Reza Mirsadeghi

Copyright © 2025 Firouz Media

All rights reserved, including right to reproduce this book, or portions thereof in any form whatsoever. For information, please write to contact@firouzmedia.com

Author: Seyed Reza Mirsadeghi
Cover Designer: Sadaf Motaghi
ISBN: 978-1-915557-27-8

www.firouzmedia.com/silence

I set free all my love, emotions, and thoughts, allowing them to flow from the gutter of my pen onto the expanse of the paper.
You, simply behold my eyes and see for yourself...

Table of Contents

Part One | The Rhythm of Awakening – 9
Part Two | A Few Breaths of Fresh Perspective – 69
Part Three | Laments in the Ruins of Time – 125
Final Part | The Passing Shadows – 189

| Part One |
The Rhythm of Awakening

Awareness and Perfection

I remember when I was a child, I was so free. Childhood had its own world. Before I learned to speak, I had already started walking! I was like a tiny sponge, trying to absorb everything.

As a child, I was completely pure and unembellished. I never pretended to be something I wasn't. I wanted to play, explore, and be happy.

I followed my emotions. I only wanted to do what I felt like doing and tried to avoid what I didn't like. All my attention was focused on my feelings, and I could even sense the emotions of others. We could call it instinct! But I think it was a kind of insight.

I was drawn to some people because I trusted them. I stayed away from others because I didn't feel comfortable around them. I had all kinds of feelings I couldn't explain—of course, because I didn't yet know words.

When I woke up and saw my mother's face, I wanted to throw myself into her arms with a fiery passion. I didn't know this feeling was called "love." Liking things… that was natural. I had the same feelings for my toys. I remember the joy and excitement I felt when my father came home from work, smiling at him as he walked through the door.

Everything was completely authentic. I didn't care about what others thought, and I was just myself because I wasn't aware of anything else. My mind had no plans. I didn't know what I was, and I didn't care to find out.

I was all purity and sincerity. This was my true nature before I learned to speak. As I delved into the memories of my childhood, I realized that, over time, transformations occurred within all of us. These transformations were the gradual emergence of knowledge and awareness.

I can recall the moment I began learning words. I learned the names of everything I envisioned in my mind. Mastering my mother tongue was an extraordinary experience.

Suddenly, I could use words to express my desires. Not long after, my mind developed enough to grasp complex concepts, and with those concepts, something incredible began to unfold.

I started categorizing everything, weaving stories: what is right or wrong, what I should do or avoid, what is good or bad, what is beautiful or ugly. I learned not just from the words my parents spoke but also from their actions. I discovered how to interact with others, mirroring everything I observed. I saw my father's strength and his firm beliefs, and I longed to be like him. It was hard for me to wait until I grew up to have my own opinions.

When I finally mastered language, the people around me began to talk about who I was. Through listening to my mother, my father, and my siblings' imagined notions about *me*, I began to learn things about myself from their perspective. And I believed them. That was the very first image of myself that started to take shape in my mind.

Because, undoubtedly, they knew more than I did—even though I was the one living inside this physical body. None of it made logical sense, but it was entertaining!

Later, when I went to school, my teacher also told me who I was. That part was fine—until the teacher began to tell me how I should be. But I wasn't like that. Yet I accepted it... and that's where the problem began. I heard the teacher say, "Children, you must work hard to become someone and succeed in life. The world is divided into winners and losers, and you are here to prepare yourself to be a winner. If you work hard, you can become a doctor, an engineer, or a lawyer in the future."

The teacher spoke about ancient kings and what they did as children. Of course, all the heroes were "winners."

I was just a child—pure and innocent—and I learned the concept of being a "winner." I made a pact with myself that I must be a winner, and that pact was stored in my memory.

At home, I heard my parents say, "Behave like this so you'll be a good boy," which meant that if I didn't act the way they said, I wasn't a good boy. Of course, they never said it outright, but that's how I interpreted it.

Now that I think about it, I realize how complicated it was! I mean, I was small—so very small—and they were so big!

If I defied them, I would fail, and they would win. I began to pretend to be something I wasn't, in order to be praised and even rewarded. I had to be what they wanted me to be, because rewards were only given to the good boys!

I remember working hard to be the person they wanted me to be. Only to hear the phrase, "You're a good boy!" What I didn't understand was the hidden message behind it, the silent messages that were never spoken but that I could still grasp. It was the message that "being myself" wasn't enough. If the message was that I had to work hard to become someone, then it meant that, at that moment, I was no one. The silent message I received from my child's mind was that I wasn't good enough! And not only that, I would never be good enough! Because I was not perfect. I accepted this idea, and at that moment, like most people, I began to search for "perfection."

Thus, the image of "perfection" was formed in my mind. I gave up being myself and began to pretend to be what I wasn't. This was my first lie, which occurred almost in those early school years.

I was a six-year-old boy, tall and thin, sitting in class, gazing at the teacher, whom I had grown quite fond of. The teacher was an "adult," so everything she said was the truth, just like everything my parents said was true. The messages I received from her were positive, but the consequences were a little different. Behind those messages was a very subtle point. Somewhere, I heard this state called "The Lie of My Imperfection," and I now use this term. This was the main lie I agreed upon about myself, and following this lie, other lies emerged to confirm and support the first one!

This was the moment of my downfall—the moment I began to be cast out of paradise. The moment my belief in the lie revealed its magic. Just like a miracle, it started to influence my entire being. I had to work hard to be good enough for my parents, my older siblings, and my teachers. It was a difficult task, exhausting, but it wasn't over yet.

When I turned on the TV, it told me how I should watch it, how I should dress, and essentially, how I should be—but I wasn't like that! The TV created other things in my mind, giving me images of heroes and villains. I saw people working hard to be winners. I saw them struggling for perfection, wanting to be important, wanting to be something they weren't.

The real dilemma started when I became a teenager. Because

by then, I knew I wasn't good enough for myself, and the result was a lack of self-belief. I tried to prove my worth to myself by getting perfect grades in school. I worked hard to be the best. At first, it was to impress my parents and those around me, but later, it was to impress myself. At this stage, I had lost the authenticity I once had. I had lost my sincerity and originality. I no longer made decisions based on what was best for me. Pleasing others had become more important.

When I finished elementary school, they told me, "You're not a child anymore, and you shouldn't behave like one. Now, you should act this way." Again and again, I tried to keep people happy by pretending to be something I wasn't. Now, I was seeking the opinions of others about myself.

How do I appear? What do they think of me? Did I do well in their eyes? I was constantly seeking validation from others. I wanted someone to tell me, "You're so good," and if I was around someone who said how great I was, that person could easily influence my life, because I needed their praise. I needed someone to tell me how smart I was, how extraordinary I was, how successful I was.

When I was alone, I tried to avoid self-judgment because I wasn't the person I thought I should be. My inner desire made me compare myself to others, and that would make me feel a little better. But then, when I looked at myself in the mirror—oh! I hated everything I saw. It was clear that I didn't love myself, but I pretended I did, and with enough practice, I even started to believe that pretense.

Later, when I really tried to prove myself to society, I became a civil engineer. Did becoming an engineer finally make me a "winner"? No! Of course not! It wasn't enough. There were plenty of engineers in society. Then, I became a well-known and somewhat special engineer with a unique approach to my work. But I still wasn't "good enough" according to the story I had in my mind.

When I was alone, I had an image of myself that I believed in. And when I was with others, I would project different versions of myself based on what others thought of me. I had to be smart enough to keep up with all my lies! I kept pretending, and after years and years of practice, I became a great actor. If my heart broke, I would tell myself: "It doesn't matter, it doesn't hurt." I lied. I pretended. I could almost win an Oscar for my performance. What a character! What a dramatic story! And I can say the drama of my life began when I agreed that I wasn't good enough.

When I heard my teachers, my family, my society telling me: "You should be like this," but I wasn't! I was in search of recognition and the acceptance of love, unaware that it was just a story! I was chasing perfection, and it fascinated me how people used the excuse of "imperfection" to justify their behavior. Every time they made a mistake and wanted to defend their image, I would hear them say: "Well, I'm just human, I'm not perfect, only God is perfect."

Then, every time I made a mistake, my favorite excuse was: "Well, no one is perfect." What a charming justification!

In my adolescence and young adulthood, during a time when my country was engulfed in an all-out war, the value of life in its spiritual meaning became more evident. I would visit mosques and religious gatherings, study the lives of the great religious figures, and I was told that this was the path to perfection. Following in their footsteps would lead me to perfection. But I found more pain and suffering in their ideology. Oh!

So, I was here to suffer, and if I endured the pain with patience, perhaps when I die, I would receive my reward in heaven. Perhaps then I would become perfect! I believed that. Because I heard it so often. But this was only one side of the story. I had delusions about myself and everything in my mind.

Even now, the lies from thousands of years ago continue to shape the stories and narratives we create. What we were told as children, as teenagers, and even as young adults, was that only God is perfect. All of God's creations are perfect—except for humans.

At that time, they also said that God made humans the most honored of all creations. But how can a human be the most honored creation, yet all other creations be more perfect than humans? I couldn't understand. After I grew older, I thought about this contradiction. It's impossible. If God is perfect, it's because He created everything. But I truly believe that God's creations are perfect. So, I think either we are all perfect, or God Himself is not perfect!

I love all of God's creations and I respect them. How can I say, "God, you created millions of humans, and none of them are perfect?" To me, saying "I am not perfect" or "You are not perfect" is the greatest insult to God. If we don't see perfection, it's because all our attention is focused on the lies—on the perfection we'll never attain.

In the end, how many of us give up on striving for perfection and, in the process, become combative? We just accept that we have failed, that we will never succeed, and then blame every external factor. There are hundreds of excuses. With this belief, "self-judgment" becomes even worse than before. When we continue to strive for perfection, we're still engaged in self-judgment, but it's worse when we give up. At that point, we try to cover up our failure and say, "I'm fine. This is the life I want," but deep down, we know we've failed. We can't hide from ourselves!

It's true… every time we try to be something we're not, we fail. It's so difficult to be something you're not, to pretend to be something you're not. I used to pretend to be happy, strong, and important! Such a life is a contractual existence with no winner. You can never be something you're not, and that's the crux of the issue. You can only be yourself, right now, as you are, and there's no problem with that. There's no need to justify who we are. We don't need to put all our efforts into becoming something we're not. We just need to return to our completeness and authenticity, to a state we had before we learned language—a "perfect human."

When we're children, we're authentic. When we're hungry, we just want to eat. When we're tired, we just want to rest. The only time that is real for us is the present moment; we don't care about the past, nor are we worried about the future. We don't enjoy life, but we like to explore and be happy. No one teaches us to be this way; we were born this way.

We are born of truth, but we grow in the belief of lies. This is the entire sorrow of humanity, the whole problem lies in the fabrications. One of the greatest lies in the story of humanity is the lie of our incompleteness. This lie has had a profound impact on my life, and although I tell others not to indulge in illusions, I myself believe that, in some way, this will happen to all of us. Of course, the stories differ, but I think that for the most part, they are more or less the same for everyone. It's hard for anyone to escape this flow. I was a complete child. I was innocent and swallowed the lie of what I should be but am not. I believed that I must strive to become what I should be. This is how I learned to create my own story. This imaginary story became my truth, and although it is full of lies, it is complete. It's very interesting and beautiful. The story is neither right nor wrong, neither good nor bad; it is just a story, that's all. But with attention and awareness, we can change the story. Step by step, we can return to the truth of existence. Because in God's creation, everything is complete. If we do not see our completeness, it is because our attention is focused on our story. The lies of our tale prevent us from seeing the truth. Yes, "with awareness, we can change the story and return to the truth."

Loving and Being Loved

A human baby is a helpless, almost ignorant, dependent, and vulnerable creature, and knows nothing of "love." If left alone before the age of six or seven, it is likely to die.

Compared to other creatures, a human can continue living independently from others much later, and it seems that with the increasing complexity of modern societies, reaching the age of independence is delayed, to the point where even if a person achieves economic independence, they remain emotionally dependent for the rest of their life.

With the growth of the child, the world around them teaches them the meaning of love. At first, the child is still small. When hungry, lonely, in pain, or distressed, they cry. Their cry usually elicits a response. Someone comes along and puts food in their mouth, hugs them to alleviate loneliness, and reduces or eliminates the source of their pain so that comfort can replace it.

These are the first contacts that teach the child to identify with another person. But this is not "love." It is dependency for the fulfillment of needs. However, this connection, simple and one-sided at first, eventually leads to the complex, multidimensional phenomenon of love.

At this stage, the way the person the child is dependent on perceives and responds to them plays a key role. But that person also has needs, and they respond to the child based on their own needs.

As the child grows, their world and dependencies grow as well. Their world of love is still limited to family—father, brothers, sisters, and most of all, their mother. Each family member, in turn, teaches the child something about love, whether through caregiving, drying and cleaning the child, playing with them, talking to them, or their responses to the child.

None of the family members intentionally sit down to teach the child the lesson of "love." There is no doubt that love is an emotional feeling, but it is also a reaction or response to an emotional state. Each family member can only teach what they themselves understand about love.

In addition to family members, there are other influential factors in the child's life that teach love. The impact of these factors can be very significant. One of these factors is culture. In many cases, it is culture that has taught the family how to respond to love. There is no one who has completely freed themselves from the influence of culture and cultural pressures.

I have always believed that if someone wants to be an accepted citizen of society, they must always sacrifice a part of themselves, lose a part of themselves. Because we must believe that if we want to be members of this society and culture, society and culture have the power to influence our thoughts, limit our choices, shape our behavior, and provide us with a definition of conformity and adaptation, showing us what they think 'love' is.

Therefore, the way we learn love is partly determined by the culture in which we live.

Fathers, mothers, and teachers (of course, fathers and mothers are the first and most influential teachers) cannot teach anything beyond what they have learned about love. This is because they themselves have been under the emotional teachings of their own teachers and culture.

If the love that teachers have learned is immature, confused, possessive, destructive, and exclusive, they will teach this same love to their young children. However, if they recognize a love that is nurturing, free, and mature, they will teach this love to their children.

A child cannot resist their teachers. They either lack the power to confront them or, if they do have it, it is very minimal and insignificant. They do not have much knowledge and do not know anything to compare with. A world is spoon-fed to them, and they are given the tools to face the demands of the world, learning how to be a loving human being, specifically.

Language, the primary tool for transmitting knowledge, perceptions, biases, emotions, and the aspects that make personality and culture unique, is taught within the family and society. By the age of three or four, a child speaks the language of their culture in an understandable way, learns its linguistic system and tone, and this is done orally because they cannot read yet.

They do not realize that the language they are learning determines what they will become, and it will influence their worldview, how they organize it, and how they present their world to others.

Every 'word' has a comprehensible meaning, but each word also carries an emotional concept. Defining a house is not difficult, but when asked to talk about the first home you remember, it becomes a completely different task. We are all familiar with the superficial meaning of the word 'freedom.' However, if we try to define freedom with our own words in the current environmental context, we will encounter conceptual difficulties. Therefore, through words, a child learns not only content but also perspective. Their attitude towards love also develops in this way. What determines the role of a child depends on how much the signs represent reality. How much these signs are analyzed, absorbed, and energized through experience.

So, 'language' is important; for creating behavior, relationships, thinking, empathy, responsibility, trust, assurance, attention, care, happiness, reaction, and in other words, the language of love is shaped this way.

From that moment on, the child, due to their lack of experience and dependence, must trust their teachers and accept the world of love they present as the reality of love.

During this time, the child begins their journey in school. There is great hope and potential hidden in the process of learning. Through education, the child faces their first form of escape. They encounter vast new needs that must be discovered, including a world filled with perceptions, different and astonishing definitions of love and life.

But, soon enough, they emerge from the "illusion." Instead of feeling the freedom to explore their own world, they begin to adopt new definitions of love and life. They find themselves in an environment that offers less flexibility than the comfort of home. While the school might not have the same strict laws as elsewhere, the experience of school becomes a compulsory one, and not conforming to it is considered a violation.

In this way, the child is essentially imprisoned within the school system. Formal education takes on the fundamental role of passing on the accumulated knowledge of the past. However, it comes at a high cost—the neglect of both the present and the future.

This method of education is more about filling the student with information than guiding and directing them toward their future. Apparently, everything, except what is essential for nurturing themselves and their relationships with others, is taught to them.

The student finds their teachers cold and soulless—people devoid of passion, joy, and hope.

Indeed, neither self-love—what education specialists call self-esteem—nor love for others, or how to love others, can be found in our current educational system.

Teachers of this time are more preoccupied with sorting out chaos—both personal and organizational—than with being creative.

Thus, the child, now fully grown, finds school to be a chaotic, vague, angry, and alienating environment, filled with meaningless facts under the guise of education.

They don't know who they are, where they are, or how they got here. They have no concept of where they are headed, nor how to reach their destination, and they don't know what they will do once they arrive.

They don't know what they have or what they want, nor how to expand and develop these desires. In this state, they are like a robot. Long before reaching old age, they are already aged, living in the past and fearing the future. In fact, they are like the teachers who have raised them in this way.

Along this path, they have never been directly confronted with love as a "learnable phenomenon."

Their knowledge and awareness of love have come indirectly, by chance, and through trial and error. The most they know about love—perhaps the only thing they know—has been acquired through newspapers and mass media, which have always exploited love to serve their own agendas. Their conception of love is never deeper than the familiar tale of a boy and girl who meet each other. One causes the other pain, a distance forms between them, and then, under the influence of the magical twists of fate and the whims of destiny, they find new perspectives and are reunited, living happily ever after. The themes of love in romantic stories are usually no deeper than this, a repetitive tale with different shades!

Commercial advertisements, mouth fresheners, cigarettes, and cosmetic companies also play a significant role in reinforcing this misguided concept of love. They assure you that love means running together in a meadow, lighting two cigarettes in the dark, or using body spray every day. They instill the idea that love arrives suddenly, often at first sight, and that you will fall in love instantly. It's all about knowing the rules of the game—no need to struggle or work for love. Love doesn't require a master; it comes by itself!

If you understand the rules, and know how to play the game, love will find you...

We often partner with those who are experts in their fields, the specialists, the efficient ones. Yet, how often do we find ourselves entangled in romantic relationships with those who know little about love, hoping—foolishly, perhaps—for something lasting, something eternal? We confuse love with attraction, with need, with a sense of security, an exciting adventure, a fleeting sexual encounter, or a hundred other transient desires.

And so, most of us never truly learn love. We entertain it, we mimic its gestures, we pretend to understand it, but we never truly learn it. We play at love, as if it were a game—perhaps because, somewhere deep inside, we know that the infinite power of love is hidden within us, waiting to be discovered, to be nurtured, to grow.

It is never too late to learn what you are capable of learning. If you wish to understand love, you must first ask: What is love? What are the qualities that make a person a true lover? How do these qualities evolve within us? The truth is, anyone can love. Every soul has the potential to love, but that potential will not awaken on its own. It requires effort, but effort does not always mean pain. It means choice, it means action—it means reaching within and beyond yourself to discover the depths of what you are capable of.

Love is learned in wonder, in joy, in tranquility, and in the heart of life itself. For the truth remains that the human soul always longs to love, and to be loved in return.

The Deceptive Mind

The moment when the truth touched my soul was during a night spent near the small town of Zabol, in a dam construction camp. It was late summer, the heat heavy in the air, and the quiet whisper of a sandstorm. Sleep eluded me, so I decided to step out of the guest room. When the storm died down, I followed the sound of a dutar being played by the site guard.

It was the first night of the month, and as I stood there, I could see millions of stars scattered across the sky. Alone in the desert, I was witness to such beauty. Among the endless stars, I saw eternity and immortality, and without a doubt, I knew the stars were alive. I knew that all of creation was alive. They were all one living entity.

Certainly, I had seen those stars before, but never in this way, never with this perspective. The sensation that seeped into me was strange—a feeling of boundless joy paired with an unparalleled peace that enveloped my being. I remember how, suddenly, something unbelievable happened. I felt as if I were no longer alone in the desert. During the time I spent observing and attempting to comprehend the vastness of the infinite, I realized that the infinite was perceiving me.

I felt as if the universe itself was aware of my existence, as if it recognized my life in a way beyond the ordinary.

That night, I realized that the infinite within my body was exactly the continuation of the infinity around me. I was a small part of it. We are all one because we are all created from light. Light manifests itself in millions of different forms to create the material world, and beyond that, I understood that there is only one force that changes everything and sets it in motion. The force that moves the stars is the same force that shifts the atoms in my body. And the driving force behind this movement is life itself—light, for light is constantly sending information to all living beings. It was unbelievable to me that I realized light is alive. Light is a living entity that holds all the wisdom of the universe within it. That night, I felt the presence of the "Almighty" with every fiber of my being.

A while ago, someone told me: "Each person is a world." And this is true. You live in your own world, and that world is very personal. No one knows what you have in your world. Only you know, and sometimes, not even you know!

Your world is your creation, and it is a masterpiece of art. That night, in the desert of Sistan, my understanding of myself and humanity shifted. My perception of the entire world changed.

In a moment of inspiration, I saw the "infinite," I saw the life force in action. That force is always present, and for anyone who truly wants to see, it is clear and undeniable. Yet, until that moment, with the focus I had on the "lies," I couldn't see it at all. It took me a long time to understand, but I finally realized it when I experienced this truth for myself. I came to understand that I am whole because I am inseparable from the life force that created the stars and all the light of the universe, from the infinite.

I am the creation of God, and I have no need for what I am not. This was my reunion with love. I regained my authenticity. In that moment of inspiration, everything made sense to me without having to think about it. I was completely immersed in attention and focus. I perceived with my soul and tried not to use words to explain it because I knew the experience would vanish if I did.

I believe that when everyone sees the truth, they are in moments of inspiration. These moments usually arise when the mind is at peace. Of course, the voice in our heads—what we've named "thinking"—almost immediately invalidates our experiences. These voices try to judge and deny what we truly feel. Why? Because when we witness the truth, none of the lies we hold onto can survive. People are afraid of the truth. That night in the desert, I was not afraid, but when I returned to my usual state, I felt fear, because I thought nothing in my life story mattered anymore.

But I had to play a part in this world. Later, I discovered that I could rewrite my life's story. I could preserve the structure of what I believed and rebuild it without lies. Life went on, as it had before, but the lies no longer ruled my existence.

Creation continues, with no end in sight, unfolding in every moment. There is always a struggle, between truth and what is called falsehood, and this is not a new concept. For thousands of years, the great leaders of religions have proclaimed, on behalf of God, that one day you will know the truth, and the truth will set you free. Free from what? Free from all the lies!

Especially from the lies that reside in your mind, constantly speaking falsehoods, which we call "thought"! Yes, the voice you hear in your mind does not mean you are hearing the truth. All it takes is not to believe the voice, and then, the voice will have no power over you anymore.

I watched the film *A Beautiful Mind* years ago, and that movie beautifully illustrated this idea.

At first, I thought I was watching yet another spy film, but when I realized that the main character was suffering from schizophrenia (split personality), the topic became even more fascinating for me. He is a very intelligent man, a genius, but he sees people who don't actually exist. These people control his life because he listens to their opinions. He has no idea that he is delusional until his wife has him admitted to a psychiatric hospital, where they diagnose him with schizophrenia and start treating him. After the treatment, the hallucinations disappear, but the side effects of the medication remain, and he decides to stop taking the medication. Without the drugs, the hallucinations return, and he comes to believe that no one else can see the people he sees. Now, he must make a choice: either return to the hospital, lose his wife, and accept that he is mentally ill, or face the hallucinations and try to overcome them.

When he finally becomes aware that the people he sees are not real, he makes a very wise decision. He tells himself, "I will no longer pay attention to them. I will no longer believe their words." Once he no longer believes in the hallucinations, their power over him fades away. With this realization, he finds peace. After many years of ignoring them, the delusions barely speak to him anymore. Though he still sees them, they no longer waste their time trying to communicate because, after all, he doesn't listen to them.

This film is extraordinary because it shows that if you stop believing the voice in your head, it loses its influence over you, and you return to your true self. The voice inside your head is not real, but it rules your life like a tyrant!

Have you ever thought about how many times you wanted to say "no," but the voice in your head made you say "yes"? Or the other way around? How many times has it made you doubt the things you truly feel in your heart? How many opportunities in your life have you missed because of fear—fear that was a reaction to the beliefs of the voice inside your head? How many times have you tried to control the people you love because you acted on the commands of that voice? How many times have you gotten angry, felt jealous, or lost control, hurting those you love, simply because you believed the voice?

The voice asks you to do many things that go against your own well-being. It's much like the mental delusions of the character in that movie. The only difference between us and that man is that while you might not see those illusions, you still hear the voice. It's incredibly tormenting. The voice never lets go, and we pretend we're mentally stable.

The voice continuously repeats its opinions and ideas, competing fiercely in our minds for our attention, constantly shifting from one moment to the next. I compare the voice of "awareness" to a wild horse that takes you wherever it wants, and you have no control over it. But it can be tamed—or at least, we can try to ride it, making that thought a tool that helps us go wherever we want.

If we don't believe the voice, it gradually grows quieter, talking to us less and less, until, eventually, it stops speaking altogether.

When we dislike someone, we can distance ourselves from them, but when we dislike ourselves, we can't escape. No matter where we go, we are always with ourselves! That's why some people try to numb themselves with alcohol or drugs, or perhaps gamble to forget who they are with. Of course, this doesn't work; it only leads to more shame and projection.

In India, people meditate and recite mantras to stop their inner dialogue. The peace of mind they achieve is incredible. Imagine being in an environment where the constant sound of beep beep beep fills the air. There comes a moment when you no longer notice the sound. You know something is bothering you, but you don't know what it is. When the sound stops, you become aware of the silence and feel a sense of relief. This is how it feels when the voice in your head finally ceases, and that is what "inner peace" means. This is how I was taught.

Let me put it another way: When someone lies to you, and you know what they said is a lie, what happens? It doesn't affect you because you believe it's a lie. If you don't believe it, the lie can no longer find a place in your skeptical mind. We know that the seemingly "aware" voice in our minds lives with us, and we know it lies to us. This is why we must stop it from speaking so that lies no longer rule our lives. From then on, we return to our true, pure selves.

But… how can we know what the truth is when almost everything we've learned is a lie? How can we discern what is real within us?

Transformation to Liberation

Some individuals, in terms of consciousness, are transported to another realm. Some suddenly feel that they have awakened. This sudden awakening comes from the questions they ask themselves or those that are asked of them, leading them to awakening and awareness. Mental processes are activated within them. They suddenly enter the world of experience. Their epistemological standards shift.

They move from "narrative" to "reason." The sanctity of beliefs and their dominance in the mind breaks. They step into another realm. They choose a different path. They begin a new journey. They realize that humans have been deceived by fear. The imposition of delusions and superstitions stems from fear. When we are freed from fear, the path to reality opens. Once the path to seeing reality is cleared, a person experiences less fear. These two are deeply interconnected.

However, I must also say that these mental and even biochemical processes that follow must be stabilized and established. This is because you sometimes see these individuals in doubt and uncertainty. In other words, inherited knowledge doesn't let go of them, causing them to feel unsteady. Breaking away from and abandoning inherited beliefs creates intense emotions and feelings. To neutralize these harmful emotions, awareness is needed. Therefore, "continuity" of awareness and mindfulness is essential.

But not everyone is like this. Many do not have access to these awakenings to become aware. They continue to follow the inherited life. Many are exposed to these awakenings but do not take them seriously. They prefer "sleep" to wakefulness. They do not want to awaken.

The numbness of the mind and repeating a symphony is their entire life. They do not want to hear or play a different melody. Therefore, the mental and spiritual state of individuals also affects their thought orientation in life. It influences their life philosophy, which is embedded in the biochemistry of their brain.

The way in which my words, breath, psyche, mind, memory, values, identity, hatred, pride, nervousness, self-assertion, and similar concepts are all interwoven makes it difficult for one to fully detach. This "detachment" has been the core issue for humans throughout all eras, and various factors strengthen and solidify this identity-building.

In fact, this very "ignorance" is humanity's affliction, preventing the path to light and awakening. It keeps one exactly where they are. Ignorance is a multi-headed serpent. We cannot simply pass by it casually.

Let us remember: for some, maintaining ignorance is seen as their "mission"!

They dedicate their entire lives to preserving and guarding ignorance within themselves! And they welcome any kind of struggle along this path.

Moreover, the problem of change lies within the "software" of the mind. When we accept that we are nothing but pre-filled software, and that clearing or erasing it is not so simple, we let go of naïve optimism and simplistic thinking. We move beyond dogmatism and rigidity. We set aside ego and pride, and discard naïve certainty. We shake ourselves awake and embark on a journey whose goal is nothing other than self-knowledge.

Where this journey leads, I do not know, but I do know that life means: continuous movement, persistence, and constant self-awareness. It's not something that will be completed in a single night.

I really don't know if things will get harder or not! Whoever seeks the truth must be diligent and awake. They can find peace right where they are. In this case, they won't face problems. The one who seeks truth must move deeply, broadly, and impartially. They must be a witness, an analyzer. Otherwise, they are merely playing games with themselves and others. These games must stop so that the person can find their way to the truth.

No one claims that we can truly reach the truth. The first step is confronting the bare realities of life. In this way, we gain the courage to critique ourselves or transcend the mind. When we see that with this conditioned mind, we won't get anywhere, we become aware of other pathways and step toward a different horizon.

Loneliness

the feeling and knowledge that human is alone, alienated from the world and from oneself—is not unique to a particular group. All humans, at certain moments in their lives, experience loneliness and are truly alone.

To live is to separate from what we were in order to reach what we will mysteriously become in the future.

Loneliness is the deepest reality in the human condition.

The human being is the only creature who knows that they are alone and the only creature who seeks another.

Their nature holds the desire and thirst to realize themselves in the other. When they become aware of themselves, they are also aware of the absence of the other, that is, of their loneliness. The fetus is one with the surrounding world; it has raw, pure life, unaware of itself.

When we are born, we break the threads that connect us to the blind life in the womb. We perceive this change as separation and loss, as abandonment, as a fall into a strange world. Later, this primal sense of loss transforms into the feeling of loneliness, and further still, it evolves into awareness.

We are condemned to live alone, but we are also condemned to transcend our loneliness and reconnect with the bonds that once linked us to a paradisiacal past life.

We use all our strength to free ourselves from the chains of loneliness. For this reason, our sense of loneliness carries a dual significance: on one hand, it is awareness of the self, and on the other hand, it is the desire to escape from the self.

It is said that loneliness is a form of trial and purification, at the end of which our suffering and instability vanish.

Upon exiting the labyrinth of loneliness, we reach union (which is rest and joy), completeness, and harmony with the world.

In popular belief, this duality is reflected in equating loneliness with suffering. The pain of love is the same as the pain of loneliness—union and loneliness are opposites yet complement each other.

The solitary person is isolated by God's will. Loneliness is both our crime and our absolution. It is our punishment, but at the same time, it is a sign that our separation has an end.

Human beings experience both death and birth alone. We are born alone and we die alone. When we are expelled from the womb, we begin a painful struggle that ultimately ends in death.

Does death mean a return to life, and is it prior to life?

Does death mean a return to the embryonic life where stillness and motion, day and night, time and eternity are not opposites?

Does dying mean ceasing to live as a being and finally, definitively arriving at pure existence?

Is death the truest form of life?

We know nothing, and yet, despite knowing nothing, we strive with all our being to escape the contradictions that torment us.
Everything—our awareness of self, time, logic, customs, and traditions—turns us into the lost ones of life, and yet everything also calls us to return.

What we seek from love (which is both desire and the thirst for union) is to taste a fragment of life, a fragment of true death!
We do not seek love merely for joy or solace but also to drink from that overflowing cup of life where opposites dissolve, where life and death, time and eternity merge into unity.

In our world, love is an almost unattainable experience! Everything opposes the lovers!
For a man, a woman has always been "the other"—both his opposite and his complement.

If one part of our being thirsts for union with her, another part—just as commanding—repels her.

As long as man's thinking remains this:
Woman, sometimes precious, sometimes detrimental, but always different—the situation will stay the same!
By turning woman into an object, by reshaping her to serve his interests, selfishness, torment, and even his love, man transforms her into a means for understanding and pleasure, altering the path to survival.

As Simone de Beauvoir said:
Woman is an idol, a goddess, a mother, a witch, a fairy—but she is never herself!

Thus, with this perspective, our romantic relationships are doomed from the very start—poisoned at their root.
A phantom comes between us, a shadow of the image we have crafted of the other.
When we reach out to touch, we cannot even feel her unthinking flesh, because the illusion of a submissive, compliant body always stands in the way.

And the same happens for the woman:
She always sees herself as an object, as something "other." She is never her own master, her existence split between what she truly is and what she imagines herself to be.

And this image—the illusion—is imposed on her by her family, her class, her school, her friends, her religion, and her lover. She never expresses her femininity fully, for even her femininity appears only in the form men have constructed for her.
Yes, and this has always been the affliction of love.

And this image is the projection of what her family, her class, her school, her friends, her religion, and her lover have imposed upon her. She never truly expresses her femininity, as even her femininity manifests only in the form that men have constructed for her. Yes, and this has always been the bane of love.

A woman is imprisoned within the image that a male-dominated society has imposed upon her. If we believe that love is a choice, not an accident—perhaps we could say that it is the free choice of our destiny and the discovery of the most hidden and fateful part of our being—then for a woman to pursue free choice is like breaking out of a prison.

In this state, those who have fallen in love say, "Love has made her a different person," and they are right. Love utterly transforms a woman.

Men, too, are deprived of choice. The range of their possibilities is very limited. As a child, a man discovers femininity in his mother or sisters, and beyond that, love is forbidden!

Modern life pushes his desires to the brink of excess, while simultaneously stifling them with a host of prohibitions: moral, social, and even hygienic. Desire is always followed by guilt. Everything narrows his ability to choose.

A man must align his deepest affections with the image of a woman that his social class deems acceptable. Loving someone from a different race, culture, or class is difficult—and if it does happen, it often leaves him blushing with shame. And since he is deprived of free choice, he picks a wife from among those deemed "appropriate." He never admits that he has married a woman he does not love.

Society equates love with marriage. Any deviation from this rule is punished, and the severity of the punishment depends on time and place, for society demands behavioral discipline from its members.

In my view, supporting marriage would only be justified if society and culture allowed for free choice. But since they do not, society must acknowledge that marriage is not the ultimate realization of love. It is a legal, social, and economic contract.

The stability of the family depends on marriage, which serves merely as a means of supporting society and ensuring its "reproduction." Thus, marriage is inherently and profoundly conservative.

An attack on marriage is tantamount to an attack on the foundations of society, and for this very reason, love becomes an anti-social act—even if it is neither consciously nor deliberately so.

Whenever love can manifest itself within the framework of marriage, society benefits. But whenever love leads to the dissolution of a marriage, it transforms into something society cannot accept.

The Bench of Solitude

I feel like I'm left behind. I walk, but I get nowhere! Or rather, I admit—I don't want to get anywhere. I just want to reach myself, a place nearby where I can restlessly belong only to myself... Is that wrong?
Someone says: Everyone wants to reach themselves, but it's impossible. It's not always possible to make restlessness a pact!

Let's not complicate it. Let's assume it's possible, for moments, minutes, or an hour, to retreat into solitude. Like those hours on a Friday afternoon, when the day moves lazily, work is on hold, and the alleys wander in their own loneliness.

And now, here I am, sitting beside myself on the bench of solitude. I clasp my hands behind my head, lean back, close my eyes, and let my thoughts drift to the happy days of childhood… I think of the sea, the forest, and the sky. I imagine myself as a fish in a river destined to reach the sea, to experience swimming alongside the bigger ones, to glide into the deepest point of the ocean, to clothe myself in the bluest hues of water, and to not think at all!

Not even about the oil clogging arteries.
Not about bread that's stale before it's even baked.
Not about cheese so salty it sulks in the corner of the table instead of gracing it.

Not at all about the constant threats of my days… What a delightful imagination I have!

In a season where the sky is the color of Isfahan's tiles, my dreams are so wild they leap from waters and seas, reaching the forest. They turn into a leaf on the branch of an apple tree, into a shade of blue yearning for a water lily, into ivy climbing the bark of a maple, and ascending ever higher!

I ride the clouds, gliding gracefully until I become rain, falling gently over a city whose hands are parched from thirst.
Suddenly, my thoughts are swept away by the wind, and I remember that I must open my eyes, for life requires open eyes!

I open my eyes, and my state is filled with melancholy—not from anyone else, but from myself… Why? Because I can't adapt to the circumstances. Because to adapt, I either have to change myself or manipulate the circumstances in my favor. For instance, I could become the caretaker of an oppressed person and benefit from the actions of that greedy, unjust person, all while staying silent about my own dreams, thoughts, and identity—because I want to become "one of them," with a smile that is impactful.

Just a few hundred years ago—no, just fifty years ago—the world was nothing but imagination and memory. Life was so simple, and the only machine was the car.

Friends were true friends, and enemies were few. There were many clouds, and the rain had endless patience. The days of "day" arrived and never left. Snow gently covered the rooftops and streets… Respect was so abundant that even cars were considerate of each other and rarely collided!

I remember that for many years, being in love was respected. Khosrow Shakibayi's *Hamon*[1] was alive, and he would say, "This woman is mine, my love!" We, too, were moved by his brave, tender words in those years, and it made us feel so good—truly good, because when it was good, it had a beautiful ending.

It had reached a point where the wound of a friend's dagger to the flesh would heal quickly, and it had reached a point where I would never accept the idea that the home is the world of a woman and the world is the home of a man. No… the home was my world too, because back then, love was a code of honor.

Sudden misfortune does not come in a way that would double the essence of misfortune, no! If it came, it would come softly and slowly, so that the fragile, mad imagination would not break at the

---

[1] Hamoun (1989) is one of the most famous cult Iranian movies, directed by Dariush Mehrjui.

thought that Layla had become friends with Farhad! In those days, being with both Shirin and Farhad, and with Khosrow, had "order,"[1] and people, holding the nobility of both loves in their hands, would not show the disloyalty of this delicate world...

Now, the world has become a different place; so much pain, sorrow, grief, and regret walks the streets and fills the news, until we forget that even hope might keep us waiting so long that we die, that we perish from waiting! Look at the hope of Afghan, Syrian, and Palestinian children, which has aged a thousand years. Their homes are no longer even visible in their dreams!

Now, in the present, we all must be chemists and veterinarians just to pick a cup of yogurt, a block of butter, a glass of oil, a chicken leg, 50 grams of meat, or 200 grams of relatively healthy fish in a grocery store. Otherwise, in the waiting line for the doctor's office or the hospital, we must sing our lamentations so loudly that our breath goes on permanent leave. And so, reluctantly, we must still remain hopeful.

But when we give free rein to a mind whose profession is meddling, it suddenly tears the thread of dreams and writes with a Bic pen: "The era of dreams is over; be realistic." Hope and dreams, shuffling side by side in a jewelry shop window in search of a lost ring, whisper: "Are you saying we should commit suicide out of fear of death?"

A stammering mind replies, "Fear does not prevent death, but it is better to know and respect the boundaries of knowing and doing and to be realistic, not a dreamer." A passerby interjects and says, "Despite all this, we must not abandon dreams. In fact, arts like painting and cinema exist to make these dreams tangible. I heard

---

[1] Referring to Khosrow and Shirin and Layla and Majnun by Nizami Ganjavi, a 12th-century Persian poet known for his romantic epic masterpieces.

this myself from Fardin[1] in an Iranian commercial movie! Or even from a arthouse movie such as '*The Runner*' by Amir Naderi!"

And so, it is good to occasionally sit on the bench of solitude and build dreams, because at the very least, it keeps the river of our being flowing and prevents it from turning into a stagnant swamp. Because that is a truth.

In recent years of delay, we have witnessed a profound transformation in our cultural and social conditions—a transformation that had occurred some time ago in pioneering countries, the reasons for which we did not fully comprehend at the time. Now that we are experiencing it ourselves, we have come to realize the root of this change: the presence of social media networks! These networks have dissolved the boundaries between social classes, giving rise to the phenomenon of the "global village," a concept foretold years ago that has now come to fruition.

The widespread use of social media in our country, considering our cultural and local characteristics, has had significant impacts, particularly among young people. Social media has even influenced the nature of relationships between individuals, overshadowing certain societal values.

When I look at this phenomenon through a sociological lens, I notice that people have become lonelier over the years.

Although social media has made virtual communication simple and accessible, it has, in practice, led to greater loneliness among individuals. If we reflect on human behavior in public spaces—like buses and subways—over the past decade, we can see how much human interactions and relationships have faded compared to before.

---

[1] Fardin was a famous Iranian actor known for his roles in classic commercial black-and-white movies.

In the subway or on the bus, most young people are glued to their mobile phones or have headphones in, immersed in their own worlds, almost oblivious to and disconnected from their surroundings.

I see, you'd like to keep the reflective, personal tone consistent with the rest of the memoir. Here's a refined version that maintains that introspective, almost contemplative style:

A generation without aspirations, one that doesn't plan for the future or think about tomorrow—it's as if, for them, tomorrow is just another version of today. Unfortunately, this isn't something isolated to the youth. Even those of us in middle age, who are supposed to guide the younger generation, have become, to some extent, victims of the same fate. And what's more troubling is that, whether through sheer laziness or disillusionment with the state of the world, we have, in a way, become complicit in this. Silent, or mimicking what we see as a more "progressive" society, without fully understanding the consequences.

What we fail to see, or perhaps choose to ignore, is that social media and modern communication technologies have created a storm in our traditional society. They have stripped away the identity, the definitions, and the very essence of our social classes. Now, we watch as the lines between the "intellectuals" and the "ordinary," between the "uptown" and the "downtown," blur, until it's hard to distinguish them at all. These boundaries, once so clearly drawn, no longer seem to exist. Just a few years ago, they still held meaning.

But let me be clear: this isn't a criticism born of disdain. It's a critique that comes from a place of concern, a genuine reflection on how far we've come—and perhaps how far we've strayed.

How did the miracle happen?

They say that whatever you believe in, will happen. That is, you must believe with all your being! Of course, when I speak of miracles, I don't mean turning a staff into a snake or cursing to make the sea stormy. Such miracles are not for us. For us, a miracle means the occurrence of an unexpected event that benefits our lives. It means the opening of a path to happiness that we never even imagined. But these kinds of miracles, like any other miracle, require certain conditions to be met. It was the same with the prophets. They had to reach a certain level before they could perform miracles.

In our own lives, I must say that a deep belief and a persistent desire can create the conditions for any miracle we wish to occur.

The life of Anthony Robbins, the author of Awaken the Giant Within, is one of these miracles. He managed to rise from nothing to everything—achieving both material growth and spiritual success, as well as inner and outer accomplishment. This man is full of energy and never stops learning and growing. It is natural that in the life of such a person, many miracles occur.

When Anthony Robbins was a teenager from a poor family, the miracle did not come in the form of a bag full of gold falling into their home. Instead, it was when a kind person brought a gift package and food to their doorstep, with a note on it that read: "Thank you for accepting this package, and I hope one day you will gift many packages to other families."

In fact, this message was the first miracle in Anthony Robbins' life. When he responded positively and helpfully to this beautiful human message, the occurrence of subsequent miracles became inevitable.

It's not as though you can sit idly by, waiting for things to fall from the sky without effort or belief. You might say that you tried hard and worked toward the success you wanted, but it didn't happen. I would say that either you didn't move forward with deep faith and belief, or the direction you were moving in was wrong—perhaps you took a detour, or from the beginning, the path you chose wasn't suited to your personality and life. We must have a powerful and active presence despite all the obstacles, problems, and injustices in order for miracles to happen to us.

Psychologists also have a beautiful analysis on this matter. They say that if you create a mental image with deep belief and love, that image will inevitably manifest in reality, and you will achieve your goal. This is provided that you don't send out negative energy yourself and that you don't pay attention to the negative energy from others.

A very important point is that your desire and decision should not be driven by greed. Greed takes up a lot of our energy. It leads to actions that are negative and not aligned with love and sincere intent. As a result, it closes the door to miracles. As a great person once said, we should not let our heart's desires turn into heart disease!

Miracles are for clear hearts, healthy minds, and pure souls. I firmly believe in this. Even if you work hard on the negative or contrary path, you will certainly succeed, but no miracles will come your way. Because it does not lead to peace and security. Someone who moves forward with purity, deep belief, continuous effort, and without despair has a beautiful world, a world in which no wrongdoer benefits from its blessings. I believe in what I say because I have seen many examples of both sides.

True success is one where you feel peace and happiness within yourself. Many people think they are faithful, with a pure and perfect religion, but when you look inside them, you see nothing but restlessness, comparison, greed, and an attempt to destroy others...

What kind of belief leads to the ruin of a person? Additionally, in my opinion, luck is different from miracles. A miracle has clear and favorable conditions, and even after it occurs, it plays an important role in the spiritual growth of the individual. For example, if a treasure had been discovered under the ground in Anthony Robbins' house and saved them from poverty, it might have been luck. But receiving that package and the profound, thought-provoking sentence on it created the conditions for true and beautiful growth (both material and spiritual) for Anthony Robbins. Of course, sometimes certain events help a person at specific moments and make things easier for them—these can act as positive occurrences. However, a miracle is a deeper and more profound event. A miracle can bring about unbelievable or unpredictable changes and impacts.

Now, let's get to the heart of the matter: if we begin a path with a pure heart, deep belief, continuous effort, and true faith, and if we proceed with unwavering determination, we will certainly encounter signs, events, and miracles that guide us along our journey.

Psychologists refer to these topics as "parapsychology" because they cannot find a clear, scientific explanation for them, and at the same time, they cannot deny these phenomena. Jung, however, accepts many of them and believes that one day science may provide reasons for them.

For our world, it's enough to know that those who can access these signs, who feel them, and who have a mind prepared to accept them, are the ones who benefit from them. A dynamic, curious mind, full of belief and overflowing with faith—filled with a desire that is passionate and driven by enthusiasm, not by uncontrolled greed or desire. Because in such a mind, things become tarnished, and these signs and symbols can no longer find their way.

Some people believe that a strong mental belief allows us to see everything and easily achieve anything. In my opinion, this is an illusion—a deception that keeps us entertained for a while through suggestion. And when we don't reach our goal, the proponents of this path say that it's because our faith was weak or our beliefs were incomplete. While one of the essentials of this path is tireless and hopeful effort—a kind of effort that is not afraid of failure and does not become disheartened by it.

Understanding Happiness

We will have a healthy and balanced society when its individuals are mentally well and socially active. Denying the psychological issues within a society is not correct. To correct these issues, we must first recognize the problem. Only then will the process of healing be easier.

In ancient times, philosophers and writers wrote books of wisdom and advice to provide people with the necessary knowledge for achieving moral and psychological balance. However, today, these valuable books alone are not enough.

Life in our era requires more subtle awareness and skills, which can only be gained through study and experience. Access to correct information and acquiring the necessary skills for life play a major role in preventing psychological harm. Although, in addition to accurate information, finding the right solutions is also essential.

For some, happiness and bliss may mean an external event in

life—a specific condition at home, a favorable work environment, good financial status, and ultimately finding a soulmate or the kind of love that nourishes the soul.

Perhaps all of these, along with a combination of other conditions and desires, depending on one's taste and interests, could be considered the ultimate goals and dreams. Yet, it is unfortunate that none of these are truly related to real happiness. This is why even those who possess all these conditions and opportunities cannot find a true sense of happiness deep within their hearts. Even though they try hard to appear otherwise and respond to the envious glances of others!

But what is the reality of human happiness?

From ancient times to the present, many thinkers have focused their minds on human happiness, but to this day, no one has been able to define it completely, let alone provide a concrete solution for achieving it. There is no satisfactory and convincing definition of happiness. In fact, most of the important matters in life cannot be precisely defined or measured. For example, can we measure or define love, friendship, or worthiness?

Psychologists define happiness as the satisfaction with one's current state, meaning it doesn't matter whether you are happy or not, what matters is that you feel happiness, and it is this feeling that shapes happiness.

Happiness is the interpretation we create in our minds of the events, incidents, and relationships in our past, present, and future. In reality, the truth of happiness is nothing but the mental imagery we form of life's journey. In other words, there is no fixed or predetermined framework, rule, or secret to happiness that can be established. Happiness is, therefore, the perspective and attitude people have toward their surroundings, and a truly happy person is someone who has the ability to interpret the events and relationships of their life in a beautiful way. However, the important question is: Can we gain the power to control and direct the mental images we create, and more importantly, how can we visualize happiness in our minds so that we can transform it into "objective happiness" in the real world?

Happiness is relative and takes on different meanings for each individual, based on their own perspective. Since it's not within our power to shape the world exactly as we wish, at least we can choose how we want to see it. There is no need for complex philosophical reasons to achieve happiness; with simple reasons, one can be happy and share that beautiful feeling with others.

Some define happiness as peace, but how peace is achieved varies for each person. Some try to create peace by avoiding or escaping from problems, but this may only bring temporary tranquility. In everyday life, there are challenges that we inevitably face. Therefore, being prepared to confront them logically puts us in a better position and creates more lasting peace for us. While there are various perspectives on happiness, what is common across all cultures is the search for it. I believe that "the secret to happiness lies in gratitude for the things we have."

One of the challenges of humanity in the age of machines and space, and in a time when a variety of entertainment and distractions are available to modern humans, is the feeling of monotony and repetitiveness in life. It is quite surprising that as life becomes more affluent and its style more modern, this feeling of monotony and stagnation increases. In such cases, any form of novelty only has a temporary effect, and after a while, it is replaced by feelings of boredom and disheartenment.

What truly is the problem of humanity?

Is it progress? Certainly not. The problem is that humans never feel satisfied. They are always searching for something lost. The issue isn't the act of searching itself, as this pushes humans forward toward progress. The problem lies in where they search for what is lost. Humans seek happiness and inner contentment, but where can this happiness be found? What is the secret to the happiness of the truly content individuals?

I once read that both happy and unhappy people largely create their own luck through their mindset and behavior. Anyone can create a better destiny for themselves, and even the unhappy can become happy.

Happy people have a strong sense of gratitude and focus on what has gone well in their lives.

Everyone experiences bad luck at certain points in their life. A happy person, when faced with a bad event, thinks about how this situation might actually be a blessing in disguise.

Happy people don't view their life decisions as "right or wrong." Instead, they make decisions with confidence and then strive to turn every situation into a success.

Happy people work hard, but they also take time to enjoy the small joys of life.

In contrast, unlucky people often put too much pressure on themselves. They work hard for long days but feel little satisfaction with what they do.

Happy people enjoy being with others, so they value their friends and make an effort to check in with them, even if their circle of friends is small.

Happy people are very optimistic about the future, and this optimism helps their dreams come true. If you start your day with positive affirmations and focus on encouraging thoughts, over time this will become more automatic and will give you a sense of positivity and satisfaction with life.

Happy people set goals for themselves, and this helps them focus on opportunities that bring them closer to achieving those goals.

Happy people take responsibility for their failures. They understand that setbacks are part of the journey, and they use them as learning experiences rather than blaming others or external factors.

Happy people tend to focus on the positive side of their luck. They can imagine how much worse situations could have been, finding comfort and perspective in the challenges they face.

Happy people smile at life and try to create joy in others, attracting positivity in return.

Happiness is an internal feeling, and it doesn't depend on what we have, but on who we are. Those who feel a strong sense of happiness tend to be more successful in achieving their material goals as well. To strengthen this feeling, it helps to reflect on both your inner and outer blessings. This boosts your spirit and gives meaning to your existence. When this happens, the sense of happiness blossoms within, and you'll feel it deeply.

One reason why some people may not experience happy days in their lives is that they keep alive the bitter and disappointing memories of the past. They constantly remind themselves of those painful moments and prefer to be surrounded by past struggles and sorrow.

We cannot change what has already happened to us, but we can learn from it. Learning from the past doesn't mean merely recalling or repeating it, but rather being aware, awake, and avoiding past mistakes. The past is experience, and the future is about building. We should always remind ourselves: "Today is the first day of the rest of our lives, and a beautiful start to rebuild our lives."

Learning from the past means finding the useful and constructive lessons it holds, even if, at first glance, it seems filled with pain and hardship. It is about using the valuable experiences gained to give direction and purpose to life. This precious heritage should be taken seriously.

Learning from the past means accepting the origin, root, and destiny of ourselves, reconciling with our true standards, accepting the weaknesses of our parents and those who played a role in our upbringing, and forgiving those who might have caused the difficulties we are facing now.

And now, what about tomorrow...?

"Tomorrow is today." There is no tomorrow. The loss of energy, mental unrest, and worries are seen in people who focus on tomorrow. We must divide life into parts of the day and make living in the present a habit.

We should not focus on tomorrow because what makes you

happy today might not seem as pleasant tomorrow. But does that mean we shouldn't take action for tomorrow? If we want to be prepared for tomorrow in the best possible way, we must focus on today's tasks. By doing so, we will certainly be ready for tomorrow as well.

The key point is that enjoying the present does not mean forgetting the future or not planning for it. It also doesn't mean being indifferent to or forgetting our past. Rather, we should learn from the past, seize the opportunities of the present, and plan for the future. We must always remind ourselves that there is no better time than now for happiness. If not now, then when? Life is always full of challenges.

It is better to accept this reality and decide to live happily despite all these challenges. We should not wait for obstacles to be removed from our path to achieve the life we desire. Experience teaches us that life is the passage through those very things we consider barriers. This "insight" helps us realize that there is no path to happiness; "happiness, itself, is the journey."

"Happiness is a journey, not a destination."

The key to joy and the feeling of happiness is focusing the mind on the present moment. One of the fascinating things about children is that they completely immerse themselves in the present. They are fully engaged in whatever activity they are doing, whether it's riding a bicycle, drawing, or anything else. However, as we grow older, we easily lose the present moment because we focus on past problems and future concerns. We delay our pleasures and joys, waiting for a different future, unaware that...

life is very short!

In reality, all we truly possess is this moment. Our peace of mind and personal effectiveness depend on our ability to live in the present moment. Regardless of what happened yesterday or what might happen tomorrow, "the present is where you stand."

Happiness is only attainable in the present, and it has real meaning then, but sadly, few people truly enjoy the present. Most people are so immersed in financial matters that they abandon the present moment.

Money is one of the things in life to which we attach more emotions than anything else. Most people are willing to lose far more valuable things than money in order to gain more. For example, they push themselves beyond their limits, even putting their health at risk, or they lose their dignity and honor in an instant just to acquire more money.

In our society, money is often seen as a powerful force, commonly used as a standard for measuring the quality of life. Yet, many of us encounter individuals who, despite their wealth and fame, seem less happy and content than we would expect. It's surprising how many wealthy people don't experience the happiness we imagine they would.

Ancient philosophers often answered the question of whether money brings happiness by acknowledging that at least a basic level of material comfort—enough to cover food, clothing, and healthcare—is necessary. But they would quickly add that beyond this, it is a meaningful life, kindness, and healthy social relationships that are essential for true happiness.

Over the centuries, people have learned that seeking wealth and material accumulation as the path to happiness doesn't lead to fulfillment. In fact, it often amplifies feelings of fear and sadness.

This isn't to say that increasing income isn't important. What we're saying is that there is little connection between wealth and genuine happiness. While money can certainly enhance our enjoyment of life, having an abundance of it does not guarantee greater happiness.

True, lasting happiness cannot be bought with money. The problem is that the human brain becomes conditioned to positive experiences. Acquiring a large sum of money unexpectedly is exciting at first, but over time, your response to it normalizes. People get used to everything—whether the best or the worst experiences—until they become commonplace.

When basic needs like water, food, and shelter aren't met, happiness has no place. But once these needs are fulfilled, the connection between higher income and happiness diminishes. A certain level of financial stability is necessary for a sense of contentment, but earning more money often leaves less time for the activities that actually bring us satisfaction, while we spend more time on things that don't contribute to our happiness.

What's important to understand is that happiness and contentment cannot be bought with money. Factors that have been identified in research as contributing to happiness—such as love, friendship, and health—cannot be acquired through wealth.

"Happiness is something we can choose, no matter where we are." The circumstances may be what they are, but it's the way we choose to look at them that determines whether they are good or bad.

Happiness is found in the proper appreciation of what we have, whether we have much or little.

People often compare their lives to others and envy their perceived or actual happiness. This is a great mistake—to assume, from a distance, that others who might seem happy are truly content, and to wish we were in their place.

Many people fail to realize that those with fame, wealth, and luck often feel miserable, because what they have—fame, wealth, and a lavish lifestyle—are not the true sources of happiness.

We tend to compare ourselves to anyone we imagine is happier than we are. If we all understood that the lives of those we envy are often filled with pain and suffering, which we are unaware of, we would certainly never compare ourselves to them or envy their situation.

By comparing ourselves to others, we won't increase our happiness in any aspect of life. On the contrary, by refraining from comparing ourselves to those we think are luckier, we can find true happiness.

In fact, happiness stems from an individual's perception. If you were to place all your troubles on a table and then someone else came and placed theirs on the same table, you would undoubtedly prefer to take your own troubles back. If you feel like you're not a happy person, visit cancer patients, prisoners, or those in care centers, and you will quickly realize how fortunate and prosperous you are. Who knows, you might even come to appreciate how lucky you are and be grateful for what you have.

Personal success means achieving what you want. However,

some people, even though they have achieved their desires, still do not experience the peace that comes with success and do not feel happy. In fact, the mistaken belief that success equals happiness—where the two are seen as synonymous—is one of the major obstacles to achieving happiness. It's evident that no matter how much success people achieve, soon after attaining it, its novelty fades, and they will long for another success. Those who were not happy before their success will not find happiness after attaining it either; in fact, they will feel even more disheartened. This is because they have equated success with happiness. Therefore, they continue striving for more success. Because of this misconception, rather than directing their energy toward achieving happiness, they invest it in the pursuit of success, and as a result, they remain unfulfilled and frustrated.

Of course, the pursuit of happiness through material success is a legitimate and healthy desire, and a person should continue striving for it. However, one should not equate it with happiness or consider it a necessary condition for happiness. If we seek material success to enhance our sense of happiness, peace of mind, and security, it can indeed add to our sense of well-being, especially when it allows us the peace of mind to pursue higher goals. But the pursuit of material success becomes harmful when it is viewed as a goal in itself, rather than as a means to enhance happiness.

There is a confusion in some of our minds regarding how some people are born into families that provide the best opportunities for growth and development, while others are deprived of these opportunities. Moreover, the path to happiness—whatever it may be—is smooth for some and not for others.

An important point in the matter of happiness that should not be overlooked is human free will in achieving happiness. A person's will and choice play a crucial role in attaining happiness, even though there are other factors beyond our control. The fact that every human being has a degree of freedom in their life and can choose their path needs no further proof. The best evidence of human free will is the very ability to make choices.

If we accept that happiness and unhappiness are inherent, and that people are drawn to good or bad without their will or choice, we must conclude that education and upbringing are useless. Similarly, the coming of God's chosen ones, the descent of heavenly verses, advice, encouragement, reprimand, criticism, and finally, punishment and reward would all be either futile or unjust.

It is important to realize that life is more in our hands than we often think. Life is the product of the thoughts, feelings, and behaviors we engage in daily, to which we have become accustomed. We must remember that as responsible, mature individuals, we can be the creators of our own happiness, rather than waiting for it to come. In fact, relying on life's events and hoping that everything will align with our expectations and desires is like jumping into a stormy sea and hoping the water won't even make a ripple.

Everything we need for true happiness is within us, and it is our internal state that chooses whether we will be happy or not. Life is what happens from the inside out. We must understand that events, in themselves, are neither positive nor negative. It is our interpretation and perception that turns them into either positive or negative experiences. Therefore, it is up to us to create heaven or hell on earth. Only by learning how to activate our inner source of peace can we truly take control of our lives.

Happiness is the feeling of satisfaction with what we have and what we don't have. It doesn't matter how much we have; what matters is how much we enjoy it. This enjoyment is what makes us happy.

We should consider contentment with life and peace of mind as the highest state of body, spirit, and soul, and equate it with true happiness.

Happiness and contentment in life are less influenced by external factors. For example, winning a lottery — as an external factor — brings a surge of happiness, but after a while, that initial overwhelming happiness fades. This is also often true for negative events such as a serious accident. The individual who is injured, after a period of time, regains hope and a desire for life, gradually returning to their former state. Thus, contentment in life is not an unchangeable state. With a change in our environment, our perception of it, and our habits and behaviors, our sense of happiness can shift and either increase or decrease.

Therefore, try right here and now to enjoy what you have because you deserve it. Life satisfaction truly gives us more enthusiasm to work hard and improve. While dissatisfaction with life can have a negative effect, leading to depression, despair, and frustration.

We are all influenced by those around us and their behavior. So, it's essential that we make a change and alter an environment that doesn't bring us joy. Typically, we get used to our surroundings. Have you ever been forced to go to a place that had a bad smell, to the point where you felt like you were suffocating? Did you notice that after a few minutes, you no longer felt the intensity of the bad smell? If you were accidentally stuck in that place for a longer time, you might not even notice the smell anymore. This happens because of human adaptation.

Similarly, if you associate with negative, dissatisfied people — those who are always in debt and feel owed by everyone. You'll eventually adapt to that misery and think it's normal. However, if you socialize with happy, motivated people, you too will become happy and motivated, and this will feel completely natural to you.

Therefore, make the decision today to change your surroundings and join a group of positive, happy individuals.

Also, the environment around us and the people plays a significant role in our sense of peace and happiness. So, create a place that nurtures your soul and brings you peace as quickly as possible.

On the other hand, our relationship with the world around us defines the way we live, and whether we feel joy and pleasure or are dissatisfied with our circumstances. Therefore, we should strive to build strong connections and share our happiness and joy with others to receive a reciprocal response from those around us.

Job satisfaction and happiness are inseparable. Our work takes up at least a third of our daily time and, in fact, a third of our lives (or even much more). If we are satisfied with our job, we have energy during our free time, but if we are dissatisfied, we become disturbed, and all the loving feelings that warm us and make us happy will depart from us. One of our most important goals in life is to achieve this sense of contentment, and it is up to us to create a satisfying work situation for ourselves. No matter what job we have, we owe it to ourselves to enjoy what we do, and this is something we are capable of achieving.

Satisfaction is a state of mind. Your mindset is something that you own and have complete control over. You can decide to enjoy your work and find ways to make that enjoyment possible. You are likely to be more satisfied with a job that naturally aligns with your nature, where your talents or passions are involved.

When you choose a job that doesn't align with your nature, you create emotional and mental discomfort for yourself. However, by maintaining a positive mindset and gaining experience, you can counteract these discomforts. One strategy is to adapt to your environment. Think of your workplace as your second home, and make it a place you enjoy by implementing small changes to improve it.

Love your workspace. Your desk is yours, and you have the power to personalize it. Place a framed photo, a small plant, or anything that brings you satisfaction on it.

Look around and distinguish between those who enjoy their work and those who don't. What sets them apart? People with a positive mindset are happy; they take corrective actions to achieve their goals. They strive—enthusiastically—to gain more knowledge about their work to improve their efficiency and increase their own satisfaction.

On the other hand, those who are unhappy cling to their negative mindset, and in fact, they prefer it that way. They look for flaws in everything they see, in everyone they interact with, and they constantly complain. They have made a decision to remain dissatisfied, whether at work or elsewhere. Their negative mindset overshadows every aspect of their being.

You should not work just for material gain. A person's job cannot simply be a means to make money; money alone does not bring peace of mind. This does not mean you should ignore income or its importance, but rather that you should do your work with contentment and satisfaction.

If you bring enthusiasm and joy into your work conditions, you will reach a point where few will be able to match you.

Forgiveness and letting go are very effective factors in achieving happiness. Many people do not realize what they lose by not forgiving, and what they gain by forgiving themselves or others.

Forgiving others is important not only because it is a spiritual and virtuous act, but also because if we hold onto grudges, life becomes more difficult for us. If we don't forgive, it is actually ourselves who suffer, not the others. Grudge-bearing and regret can make us ill and seriously damage our immune system.

We all make mistakes, and we must forgive others' mistakes and not let them harm us. Forgiveness protects us from all the hatred and grudges we hold in our minds, replacing anger and hostility with a sense of peace and comfort within us.

In life, not only must we forgive others, but we must also forgive ourselves. Many people spend their whole lives punishing themselves mentally and physically for the shortcomings and mistakes they attribute to themselves. If you have felt guilty until now, enough is enough. Do not continue, for the persistence of guilt will not solve any problems. Try to release this feeling from yourself.

We are always drawn toward the things we think about. The principle is that whatever you think about, you are drawn to it. Even if you think about things that you don't desire, you will still be drawn toward them.

The fastest and best way to create positive thinking is to use positive and empowering words. In fact, the power of words is unbelievable. A person has the ability to remove an unpleasant situation through the power of their words, transforming sorrow, depression, and illness into joy and health.

We must truly understand the weight of words. Even if they pass through our minds and language involuntarily, words like "disastrous," "bad," and "terrible" have a profoundly destructive effect.

It is important to remember that we are constantly becoming what we think about. Our thoughts influence our emotions. Thoughts not only rule our lives, but they also shape them.

We can spend our entire lives labeling events as good or bad, seeing one as a blessing and the other as a misfortune. The reason we label every incident as a disaster or a catastrophe is that we are only seeing a part of the whole reality. As long as we believe the situation is bad, no change will occur. Until we greet our days with shouting and fighting, we won't see any progress in life.

However, the moment we change our perspective on life, everything begins to shift. When things are not going as we hoped, we should realize that the events themselves may not be that important, but how we perceive and handle them is what truly matters.

All human beings, whether they adhere to religious principles or not, or regardless of their religion, are searching for better things in life. In fact, our movement and activity in life are directed toward finding joy and living happily. The pursuit of happiness, as a life goal for achieving happiness, motivates us and not only benefits the individual, but also greatly benefits the family and society the individual lives in. Therefore, it is wrong to consider this a selfish endeavor.

Although achieving happiness is possible, happiness is not a simple feeling and depends on our mindset and actions in life.

It is important to differentiate between happiness and pleasure, as they are distinct from each other. True happiness is more connected to the heart and mind, while pleasure, which is often tied to physical sensations, is fleeting. It may be present one day and gone the next.

"Happiness originates from the soul and spirit of a person, born from truth and love." Happiness cannot stem from self-centeredness or selfishness; thus, it cannot thrive alone. It seeks to include all beings on Earth in its experience. Someone who cannot look beyond their own interests will never feel true happiness. When we focus solely on our own desires and wants, we are likely to become selfish and indifferent.

Another secret to happiness is to allow benefits to spread and encompass everyone. Humans are inherently social creatures. If they are not in harmony with others, they cannot experience happiness either within themselves or in their relationships with others. Empathy for others and sharing in our joy are the foundations of humanity's survival. The true value of human life lies in this, and without it, a part of us is lost.

The time when our school was near our home, it was so large that we couldn't see the other side of the yard. Maybe I was too small, or my eyes didn't reach that far. The school was square-shaped, with two sides having a two-story building, perfectly suited for educational purposes. I was in love with the principal, who would line us up early in the morning to sing the national anthem, "Ey Iran," under the flag, sending our childish voices up to the sky.

Back then, the age gap between children in the same class

was not just a few months. Sometimes it stretched across several years! Because of this, we witnessed a wide range of educational dynamics. In the middle of elementary school, they replaced our kind-hearted school supervisor. One day, after running from home to school, in the half-dark hallway entrance, a shadowy figure blocked my way. He shouted at me, "Grab my hand." I stretched out my small hand as far as it could reach. Every inch of my child's body trembled. Even after more than 36 years, I can still feel the pain and burn of that ruler from our strict, burly supervisor.

In the fifth grade of elementary school, we had a teacher who would look into the faces and eyes of the children. If someone's face turned pale, their chin trembled, or they lowered their head, he would call them to the blackboard. When "Razeghi" was chosen, he would tremble all over. His mouth would dry up, his tongue would get stuck, and he would lose his balance, constantly saying, "It's on the tip of my tongue... Please, sir..." Sometimes, before even being punished, he would break down.

In high school, every year, one of our subjects was with Mr. Afrasiabi. He was a man who loved jokes, witty remarks, and teasing. He would often say he was in love with teaching. Mr. Afrasiabi was passionate about the rich Persian literature. Otherwise, he claimed, the profits from his own car dealership would be enough to support him many times over. In our final year of high school, he would pull out a notebook from his pocket and recite the last few lines of dictation to us. We neither understood the meaning of the words nor, if we did, did it matter. Our education was supposed to be about distinguishing whether a word had "gh" or "q," "s" or "c." During all the years we studied "History" in school, no one ever discussed with us the history of an event. The circumstances and factors that led to an event, the reality of those days, were never explored. Everything focused on "historical events" and the names, places, and outcomes—facts we would learn today and forget tomorrow.

Whenever it rained, our sports teacher would sit us in a sheltered area and give us advice. When the weather was good, they would hand us a ball and leave, off to "take care of other matters"!

I remember that a subject called physics had just been introduced into our curriculum. Our physics teacher was old, dry, and always angry. One of the kids, a curious, bold, and troublesome student, asked, "Why?" The teacher replied, "Why doesn't physics exist?" And we realized that all our physics was in the book, and sometimes on the "blackboard"!

In those days, people avoided and feared placing the "why" on their beliefs and accepted ideas. They didn't know that newcomers should be welcomed into the cities of what we had and what we knew through the gates of "why." Scholars of human sciences, educational sciences, philosophy, politics, religion, and ethics, when they met, would rise above debate and sophistry... sometimes their discussions led to accusations, insults, and even separations. Occasionally, in their efforts to either accept or reject a theory, they would turn to Persian or Arabic quotes from past or contemporary great thinkers, with or without references, to justify their words!

In school, they always recommended and praised "keeping your head down" and condemned "keeping your head in the clouds!" They didn't know that children should be raised in such a way that one eye looks at the ground, and the other looks at the faraway horizons—the unknown. A "well-behaved" child was one whose command was in the hands of the elders, not one who held the "command of life" in their own hands. Ultimately, they thought the purpose of education and upbringing was to prepare children for the "present life"—not for the "future life," a life that hasn't arrived and hasn't been experienced yet. I remember, they only asked for "knowledge" from us, not "scientific thinking."

I remember that both at school and in the neighborhood, our childish play was seen as "mischief" and often led to trouble. But today, I see my children's play as a sign of their physical and mental health, and as a tool for their cognitive, physical, emotional, and social growth.

It is truly fascinating to observe the many differing opinions about child-rearing in a developing society and across different eras.

There was a time when they thought for the child and acted in place of the child. Sometimes, their desires and wills were placed in the place of the child's. As time went on, we realized that we must place the child in front of the problem, or rather, place the problem in front of the child! We must make thinking, choosing, and deciding part of their behavioral model.

In those days, "obedience" and accepting things as they are was considered the process of "upbringing." They did not know that the development of societal education lies in understanding others and changing what is. The result of such behavior was that children, under the pressure of education, would either surrender to whatever was imposed upon them or turn their backs on everything. This was because only the words of the elders mattered, and the "judgment" of the elders was imposed upon the child. Today, we have learned that by understanding what is, we can create what should be. We must present to the child what exists, exactly as it is, and leave the judgment to them.

We now know that children are the best advisors in the home and school when it comes to understanding their world and uncovering their developmental needs.

Truly, it was a world back then that is strangely different from today! At that time, "laughter" was seen as a sign of frivolity, but today "laughter" is considered a sign of healthy thinking and psychology. I remember that back then, the elders imposed recreational tools and spaces on the children. But in this era, children's recreational tools and spaces have even sparked an interest in the older generation as well.

In those days, children's daydreaming and imagination were ridiculed and discouraged! Whereas today, all child psychologists and educators see imagination as the foundation of thought, and they encourage it. Just as everyone believed that children and adolescents should learn how to behave with their parents, today we believe that parents must learn how to behave with children, adolescents, and young adults.

Good and bad, meaning the black and white colors, were the only colors that colored the world of children in that era. Today, we try to introduce our children to a broad spectrum of colors, avoiding absolutist thinking – a wide range of "behaviors" – seeing them in their own world and trying to digest childish behavior.

At that time, we were made to understand that you could learn anything, anytime you wanted! Of course, the fear of the student was the guarantee of learning, and threats and the power of fear were the foundation of the teacher's lessons! But now we have learned that learning anything follows stages and phases, and if you miss those stages, it will not become a behavioral part of you. And of course, learning is also about co-learning, questioning, and discovering the unknown through what is already known. The result and outcome of this is participation, creativity, and innovation.

I remember when I was a teenager, in behavioral discussions, seeking advice and listening humbly to others' opinions was seen as a sign of weakness, lacking authority, power, and independence in one's actions. Decisiveness, even in doing something wrong, was considered a sign of authority. And later, we learned how much we needed to change our mental beliefs because seeking advice and opinions is a sign of strength of character and wisdom in guiding life for ambitious, responsible, and capable individuals.

What I realized from that time, and what I understood was that others were pleased with my understanding, was this: "The family" held sovereignty over "the child" — not only in eating, sleeping, sitting, standing, and studying, but also in choosing a field of study, selecting a spouse, accepting a job, choosing housing, etc. The child could not easily escape the grip of the family's desires, beliefs, and aspirations.

But in this day and age, parents and families speak with the sweetness of honesty and sincerity about their life stories, their dreams, their successes and failures, what they have gained and lost, without any manipulative adjustments. Their noble advice is this: **Do not become like us...**

Part Two
A Few Breaths of Fresh Perspective

Introduction

Despite the unprecedented development of mass media, extensive communication possibilities, the existence of virtual communication platforms, and the availability of a vast array of books—containing countless ideas, opinions, and astonishing beliefs—many of us humans merely pass by these concepts, like a pedestrian gazing at shop windows along a street. We read, listen, and quickly forget them, without seeking to embed them into our hurried lives or deeper thoughts.

The writings in this collection are the product of observations and experiences related to certain perceptions, behaviors, and issues in our society and the world around us. Some themes addressed here are more readily accessible, while others require deeper exploration behind layered concepts or a redefinition of familiar ideas.

These notes aim to open a new chapter in life by redefining a broader vision, challenging established criteria with moral courage, breaking intellectual barriers, and training ourselves to transcend idle thoughts. The ultimate goal is to elevate the level of our thinking and expand our perspective.

From a content perspective, the focus of these writings is on observing certain behaviors, actions, and words, and reflecting on spaces that often seem self-evident. Additionally, the material is presented with careful attention to concepts that lie at the intersection of two or more approaches within fields such as sociology, behavioral studies, psychology, and related disciplines.

However, I must emphasize that there is no dogmatic insistence in analyzing these interpretations. Therefore, I do not claim that these reflections are entirely flawless, accurate, or unquestionably valid.

As such, I kindly ask the reader to approach the material with a critical perspective. While some of the topics might feel familiar, or certain themes may carry a tone reminiscent of moral advice—for which I apologize in advance—I have made every effort to present these findings, many of which are informed by the teachings of esteemed scholars in conceptual sciences, in a more tangible and independent manner.

May the grace of God enable these reflections to reveal the beauty of life more vividly before our eyes and deepen our understanding in perceiving such beauty.

Single statement

When Strangers Greet with Familiar Smiles, Why Do Longtime Locals Turn Away?

…Everyone seems to be searching for someone to blame—someone responsible!

At night, fear blankets the city, and by day, it hides in the cold glare of the sun. These days, fear has become a constant presence, dark curtains shroud the windows, and smiles… are the rarest of treasures.

Worry and sorrow seem etched onto faces, as if carved in stone. Anger, accompanied by indistinct murmurs and broken smiles, lingers in the air. In this atmosphere, I find myself searching for an answer to this question.

You see… I always believe that perhaps the light hasn't been extinguished yet. Streets can still be filled with movement and life. It's possible to imagine a sky adorned with vibrant hues. The leaden clouds weighing on our minds can and must be swept away. So, we must begin with ourselves. We must breathe in a fresh perspective, take a few moments to view life anew…

A new way of thinking, after all, can be the key to living free of resentment.

A New Chapter of Life

Whenever we sit quietly by the riverbank, listening to the flow and movement of the water, we realize there is always a profound, extraordinary sense of motion—vast and deep. In contrast, a stagnant pond shows no sign of vitality; its waters are still and lifeless. And if we look closely, we understand this is often what many of us seek—a small, static pond and a life devoid of life's dynamic flow.

Wherever the current of life finds its way, it will carry you along because you are a part of it. From this perspective, the negative behaviors and words of others appear hollow and meaningless. This is the beauty of life—to break free from the stagnant pond and join the searching, exploring river of existence.

It is essential to step away from the rigid frameworks of our minds and cease measuring our humanity and identity by shallow, artificial standards. And yes, doing so is no easy task.

When we are dreaming, we perceive it as absolute reality, only realizing its illusory nature upon waking. By this analogy, entering higher levels of consciousness awakens us from the slumber of ignorance, allowing us to recognize the misconceptions that have shaped our lives. From this newfound perspective, life's mysteries are revealed, and we learn to trust the "river of existence," surrendering to its flow with patience and calm.

No longer do we anxiously chase destinations or lose our peace over situations that once unsettled us. Instead, we let go. For instance, if our flight at the airport is delayed by three hours, we endure the wait with harmony and serenity, trusting in the flow of life. When events steer us away from our desires, we embrace them with the understanding that divine love is guiding us toward something more fitting and fulfilling.

We must calm ourselves to hear the voice within and feel our presence in these higher realms of consciousness. Upon entering the "realm of awareness," we find no need to judge others or pass verdicts on their lives. We awaken to the truth that criticizing others diminishes the quality of our own lives and wastes our energy. Scrutinizing and analyzing others' behavior is a destructive, antisocial act, requiring immense effort to gather evidence and craft arguments, all while eroding our inner peace.

Trusting the flow, listening to our inner voice, and releasing judgment allow us to live more freely and harmoniously within the vast river of life.

We must not forget that the word "integration" is in direct opposition to the word "fragmentation." In the process of integration, all components function as inseparable cells of a unified whole, eliminating conflict and duality. In other words, integration arises from unity, harmony, and coherence, whereas fragmentation in human behavior stems from duplicity, discord, and strife.

In an awakened society, the energy of each individual supports the energy of others, creating a collective force greater than the sum of its individual parts. In such a society, all matters are driven by collaboration, ensuring that the unemployment or hunger of one person becomes a concern for the entire community.

Selflessness and altruism are defining characteristics of an awakened society, where individuals work together in harmony to build a world where no one is left behind, and shared well-being is prioritized over personal gain.

To measure your level of altruism, observe your reaction when you see underprivileged children playing in the mud due to a lack of resources, unable to enjoy the shelter, cleanliness, and food your own children have access to. Perhaps it's time to nurture and strengthen the tendency for "sacrifice and generosity" within ourselves. This growth can open a new chapter in our lives, preparing us to embrace all the joys and wealth that life has to offer.

I believe we have the potential to become empowering, resilient, sweet, kind, and lovable individuals.

Above all, we must be in love—with life, with others, and with ourselves. And a loving person must care for and look after themselves.

This isn't about selfishness or self-indulgence. A loving person understands that everything passes through the filter of their being. To give love and kindness to others, they must first nurture their own inner light.

The greater I grow and the more I possess, the more I give. The more knowledge I acquire, the more I feel compelled to share it. I can shape myself into the most fascinating, beautiful, awe-inspiring, and loving person on this earth.

We are merely a tiny fraction of what we could become because humans hold immense, untapped potential. It's no wonder that, if we truly desired it, we could metaphorically soar. We have extraordinary abilities—clearer vision than an eagle, a sharper sense of smell than a hunting dog, and the capacity for boundless intellect. Yet we seem forever content with the small piece of ourselves we currently know, indulging in sweet dreams of what we are, clinging to this fragment instead of reaching for the vastness of what we could become.

Psychiatrists suggest an interesting perspective: what we think is far less than what we know; what we know is far less than what we desire; and what we desire is a mere fraction of what actually exists. Thus, we are much less than the totality of our potential. Does this thought not make your head spin?

If the entire essence of life could move toward growth—toward seeing, feeling, and understanding—then not a single moment would remain for sorrow. Life would transform into an unending journey of expansion and discovery, a continuous unfolding of what it means to truly live.

Do you know, we are truly remarkable beings, and being human is the greatest blessing on Earth. And yet, we are also quite funny, and perhaps we need to relearn how to laugh. Admit it—sometimes we do absurd things. For instance, we created time, and now we've become slaves to it. Take this very moment, for example: maybe in the back of your mind, you're thinking you have only ten more minutes to finish something. You might even be in a place where something monumental is happening. Yet, when it's time to leave, you have no choice but to go.

We have alarms that constantly ring. Each time we hear one, we react instinctively. We're told where to be—here or there. Yes, I'll say it again: we created time, and now we are its servants.

The same applies to words. Language is an incredibly powerful force. A word is just a combination of letters and sounds placed together. You assign meaning to it, and then that word sticks to you. You give it a cognitive meaning, an emotional significance, and then you live by that word. Once you learn a word and its emotional and literal meanings, you remain attached to it for the rest of your life.

In this way, the world of your words is built. We use words to label things—for instance, we say, "Oh, them... ugh," and in our minds, we erase and silence them.

But we must understand that no word, no matter how vast its meaning, can ever fully capture even the simplest of human beings. Only you have the power to stop someone in their tracks, but a person who loves would never do such a thing. There are so many beautiful things within every individual that it's impossible to label them and push them aside.

A loving person has a sense of responsibility. A loving person despises waste—whether it's wasting time, opportunities, or the resources available to us.

And another thing: I believe that "this loving person lives in the moment and cherishes the beauty of existing in time." Because a loving person constantly sees the joy and wonder of being alive.

A loving person recognizes their needs. They need compassionate people, someone who is at least kind to them, someone who truly sees and hears them. Perhaps just one person, but one person who pays attention to them and cares for them. Sometimes, just one finger can cover the crack in a dam!

If you don't want to engage in pointless arguments to "make your point," find the truth in the words of the other person.

You can accept criticism without defending your mistakes, without needing to prove you're right. It may seem strange, but it's not.

I know this "law of opposites." When you agree with a critic and highlight their mistake, but when you oppose them, you only make them more convinced that their perspective is correct.

You see, the skill of listening is often underappreciated. Responding with empathy in moments of sadness or criticism, or when you feel no one is listening to you, is difficult. And unfortunately, this is exactly when you need your listening skills more than ever. Because trying to defend yourself only makes the other person more frustrated.

They, too, want to make their point, and the more you oppose them, the more determined they become to prove you're wrong.

Practice this, because I've learned this from experience!

A Grand Perspective

A skilled sculptor creates a masterpiece by following a specific pattern, chiseling, scraping, and shaping it to achieve coherence. Similarly, we, as humans, can transform our presence on this earthly planet into a legendary and imaginative work of art by changing our perspective on life's aspects and adjusting and fine-tuning its various dimensions.

To see ourselves in mutual connection with all elements and forces of life and align with our divine and human design, we must first ask ourselves: How do we wish to be remembered after our death? What acts of help, sacrifice, and success do we want to be remembered for? What differences do we wish to have made in our lives? When referring to the lives of certain individuals, who can we say led a life that was a true masterpiece?

To achieve a deep and rich life, transforming it into a unique masterpiece of art, we must make love the resident of our hearts, intertwining compassion and care with our very being. We must make helping others a core principle of our essence. Let love, compassion, forgiveness, and grace guide our actions and behavior, and in the most difficult circumstances, we must maintain our equilibrium.

Personally, several years ago, an experience transformed my thinking and my perspective. A higher level of awareness became accessible to me, and I referred to it as the "Grand Perspective." I ventured so far that I even wrote my own obituary as I desired it to be, going so far as to predict what might be said during my funeral and mourning, and I repeated it to myself for a long time.

Sometimes, the threat of illness, painful misfortunes, or severe family conflicts can expand one's horizons and lead them to a fresh awakening.

Some individuals do not need anyone to guide them in connecting with their higher wisdom and insight; they reflect on their behavior and actions, and when they spot an error, they correct it. Meanwhile, others may need to consult a counselor or a center for spiritual self-development. Some begin their journey towards transformation and higher awareness after reading books on psychology, philosophy, and metaphysics.

The method by which one reaches the 'Grand Perspective' is not what matters; what is important is that by connecting with higher levels of consciousness, we allow the infinite and boundless power within us to clear away the confusion and emotional strain from our existence.

In my travels to distant corners of the world, I open my mind to learn truths and information. For example, when I see a beggar missing a hand or a leg, I interpret it as a lesson to place generosity at the forefront of my actions. Or when I see an elderly woman driving slowly and aimlessly in front of us, I regard her as my senior teacher, in the role of someone who wants to teach me to work on my spiritual strength and not to lose my temper over trivial matters. She is trying to convey to me the importance of letting go of unnecessary agitation and excitement, calming my personality, and moving forward in harmony.

When we feel hurt by someone's behavior, if we pay attention to the fact that we are all an inseparable part of one magnificent whole, we will come to believe that this individual is but a manifestation of a part of our own being, appearing in a different form!

With this mindset, our expectations for situations and circumstances to always align with our desires and preferences will fade away.

In every relationship and situation, we should consider people as teachers who intend to teach us something. So, let us be alert to see what we can learn from them.

Finally, it would be nice to share an interesting, true, and short story! Many years ago, I worked in a company where the window of my office faced a busy main street. At that time, I was suffering from a nervous condition, and the sound of car horns severely disturbed me. One day, I suddenly lost my temper due to the continuous honking of a car outside the window, shouted a curse, and rushed towards the exit door. A colleague who witnessed this event (and has since passed away) was quietly watching me.

The next day, the same thing happened again, and I angrily said to the same colleague, 'If I ever gained power, I would remove that damn horn from the car.' He calmly responded, 'I don't think you will ever gain such power,' and as I looked at him in surprise, he completed his sentence: 'If you were endowed with magical and great power, the car's horn could not disturb you and upset you to this extent!'

With that sentence, he taught me a great lesson – may God bless his soul.

Changing Standards

In the past, we used to completely draw lines between good and bad, right and wrong, or ugly and beautiful. The books we should read and the books we should not read! The things we should do and the things we should not do. But now, at this stage of life, as I want to talk about my own tastes, joys, and personal dislikes, and simply follow my own desires, I think of all these old games! I simply think! And fortunate are those who, at any point in their life, find an opportunity to reflect on their thoughts from yesterday—which today they call old games. I want to talk about reviewing standards. A standard is a tool for measuring, for weighing our actions—not value, which should be discussed elsewhere and, of course, by other thinkers!

I want to talk about new and at least revised standards, those that we urgently need to know in order to help our work today. These are the standards that, after recognizing our capabilities, we can use to organize our lives. I am talking about social, economic, and similar standards, which, unless we reconsider them, will leave us with nothing but self-deception, even at best. I want to discuss these revisions through examples I've gathered from here and there, explaining why, as Iranians, we need to rethink many of our standards. Therefore, my words are directed somewhat to myself and to other compatriots who believe that this need for revision is a serious one. If we don't address it and remain immersed in our "knowledge," without striving to update and refresh our understanding, if we continue to delight in our eternal knowledge, the course of time will not be lenient with us. We must accept that the world is changing every moment.

They say that the speed of scientific progress, and consequently technology, almost doubles every year. Before we could fully utilize steam and energy, we could not have achieved this doubling even over two thousand years. Now, how can we expect our knowledge and standards, from forty or fifty years ago, to remain unchanged and valid in their original form?

We must accept that the world today is hundreds of years ahead of the world of fifty years ago, and most of its standards have been turned upside down. If, as a thinker, a businessman, or a politician, someone still wants to continue their work with the knowledge from fifty years ago, they will naturally never reach the desired outcome, and that is their problem.

The same goes for economic and political relations between two countries. Yes, once upon a time, the British used to officially appoint our prime ministers, but now, if they try hard enough, they might be able to pull themselves together. You see how today they are in a relatively humiliated position, trying to follow after another superpower. Today, if Britain works seriously, it may manage to place a few mid-level influencers in the countries that were once under its influence, and nothing more than that. They themselves are so tangled up in their own difficulties that they are currently occupied with them...

Don't forget, I am not trying to cleanse the sources and causes of colonialism; that's not my point. What I am trying to explain is the shift in the course of this greed. My point is that when such a foreign power-driven mindset becomes widespread in a country, any incompetent, unqualified individual appointed as the head of a small factory, employing a handful of people, will justify their shortcomings by attributing them to external factors, and blame them on invisible forces! Just as they've done until now...

Look! Up until about eighty or ninety years ago, coal played a very decisive role in balancing the power between the leading countries of that time. But we saw that this standard collapsed within about twenty or thirty years, and the era of oil began. In fact, all the major events of the 1960s and 1970s were dictated by oil dynamics—meaning that the power of coal was handed over to oil, and the strength of large military forces was directly related to controlling this vital resource. Especially in the oil-rich countries of the Middle East, where every political event, big or small, eventually ended up connected to the oil wells. Why? Because it was the most decisive factor in driving the wheels of the economy and factories.

(Don't rush!! Don't think I'm about to conclude that the era of oil has passed; rather, I'm saying that other eras have arrived, and examining them is at least worth considering...)

But still, our great leaders, politicians, and intellectuals—whether employed or not—have focused all their attention solely on this oil, making it the center of everything.

I've always wondered why we still believe that the whole world has gathered to take our oil money from us? Of course, I don't claim that we are no longer a target—yes, we are, and more intensely than before—but know that the nature of this desire has changed. If we focus all our attention on oil, they will take our minds, our athletes, our Caspian Sea water, and when that happens, we won't be able to create any added value, and we'll have lost the worth of our crude oil many times over. Pay attention—today, if these same elites are nurtured in the right environment, whatever economy you imagine, each one of them could be worth as much as an oil well. And not just in terms of extracting benefits, but we'll still leave space for Russian and Chinese companies to profit off of our oil!

With a simple calculation based on the average oil sales over the past seven years (though, of course, based on not-so-accurate information, which is now very difficult to access!), a significant portion of that income goes toward extraction, transportation, commissions, and the costly structure of the Ministry of Oil. A large portion of it is also spent on buying corn, wheat, arms, rice, oil, sugar, and fodder, and finally, some of this revenue is used for the country's infrastructure budget, electricity networks, and so on. How much do you think remains for all the imperialist countries to come together and profit from? Compare this leftover sum, which is under ten billion annually, with, for example, the one trillion-dollar exports of Germany or the approximately $500 billion U.S. military budget, or even the over $40 billion annual sales of McDonald's franchises!

What I want to conclude is that the calculations post-World War II, on which our ancestors, our rulers, based their political thoughts and, rightly so, built at the time, have now fallen apart... the colonial formulas have changed, and we need to realize this. Therefore, we must preserve our wealth-generating resources, but not only do we fail to think about utilizing these resources effectively, but by bad fortune, we also seem to be pushing them away. This program must be a long-term, well-calculated one, based on new criteria, and I insist on understanding these new standards.

In military affairs, the same thing is true: all the equations are overturned. The forty-year Cold War between the Soviet Union and the United States—symbolizing the Cold War—proves this point. The old notion of military might is outdated... the real strength now lies in electronic tools, economic power, science, information, and above all, in the minds.

Today, the same McDonald's chains, which I mentioned earlier, or similar companies, generate such income in just one month for their shareholders that Nader Shah, with all his notoriety, couldn't achieve in India from his armies, not even by shedding a drop of blood or violence...!

But still, in some corners of the world, there are many who wish to have armies of several hundred thousand men marching before them, for no reason or for any reason, unaware that in today's world, it is quite possible for an electronic eye or a satellite tool to perform the work of dozens of armies. A cruise missile, from thousands of kilometers away, can obliterate a large target with an error of only a few centimeters, all by a soldier weighing just 5 kilograms!

Therefore, the power of modern systems is not measured by the size of their populations or the number of their armies. The most determining factor is science, knowledge, wisdom.

During World War II, the Nazis in Germany besieged the city of Leningrad (St. Petersburg) for about two and a half years. A third of the city's population was killed, and the rest endured conditions far worse than death, creating a moment of horrific suffering that became a historical memory. The besiegers themselves were not in a better state. They tore open the bellies of horses, dying of starvation, in order to warm themselves with the animal's body heat to prevent freezing. But today, see how these same resilient people, with the help of McDonald's, Coca-Cola, and IBM, have opened the city to strangers and generously showered them with rubles! Observe how, in an astonishing way, the criteria have completely changed!

Therefore, it is we who must strive with all our might to survive with dignity, ensuring that our plans, actions, and decisions are not based on the outdated and obsolete "Uncle Napoleon"[1] logic. We

---

[1] The term "Uncle Napoleon" (Dai Jan Napoleon) became widely known through the Iranian TV series of the same name, which aired in 1976. The TV series, based on the story by Sadegh Hedayat, brought the character of Dai Jan Napoleon to a broader audience and further solidified the term in popular culture. In both the short story and the series, the character is depicted as a charming but deluded man who confidently offers advice and opinions on matters well beyond his understanding, often causing trouble or confusion. The TV series added a comedic element to the character, showcasing his absurd confi-

must follow current global issues but not become overly excited; we should wisely and realistically pursue our reasonable and achievable desires with open eyes.

Especially since we all know that the people of Iran usually approach social issues with their hearts and emotions, rather than adhering strictly to ideologies, party lines, or other constraints. For this reason, what works in Iran is not a "party," but a "movement," and it has always been these movements that have been influential and historically significant. This is because a movement often forms in response to saying "no" to a phenomenon, such as an organization, a trend, or even a system, and most people come together in their social institutions, spontaneously but shallowly, around a "desire," even if that desire is negative. However, to say "yes" collectively requires more than just a spontaneous reaction—it requires the aggregation and alignment of different tastes and perspectives, which, due to the severe class, cultural, and social conflicts that exist, is generally difficult to achieve easily. We don't need to look far in history, especially in the past century, to see this. In the Constitutional Revolution, rather than benefiting from the constitutional project itself, we celebrated the victory over despotism! And similarly, in the movement for the nationalization of the oil industry, the main goal seemed to be saying "no" to the British, rather than benefiting from the oil itself and channeling the revenues into the people's pockets.

The main point, however, is not to forget the need for rethinking our standards.

It was common, and still continues, that dominant countries <u>plan and draw maps to incite weaker and less powerful countries</u> dence and the resulting absurdities of his actions. Mentioning Dai Jan Napoleon refers to an outdated, often misguided way of thinking that persists despite its ineffectiveness in modern times, symbolizing the kind of false confidence in one's own limited or outdated knowledge.

against each other, in order to profit by selling military equipment. But now, gradually, methods are changing. Some time ago, I saw an intriguing image in a few emails. This image was from 2009, showing a large crowd of people dressed in black from Senegal, walking in the streets.

There were people whose faces showed signs of disease, hunger, and poverty. These images depicted a significant number of passersby holding their mobile phones to their ears, engrossed in the "delight of the ear."

It's clear that when technology allows you to make a "lightweight" phone out of a few dollars of plastic and sell it to these unfortunate souls for a hundred times its price, what need is there to make tanks, armored vehicles, or missiles and sell them, with their size, complexity, and transportation issues? Moreover, if they can profit from selling these "heavyweights," they wouldn't miss the opportunity.

In industry, it's the same. For years, the world of industry has realized that instead of concentrating a large factory in one location, they are making smaller factories, even workshops that can fit in the home of a worker, so that later, after collecting products from these small workshops, they can assemble them under one roof.

... See, just by reducing workers' hours, transportation, and compulsory payments, they save a lot and capture new markets. Now, look at the developing countries; every day, their newspapers announce the inauguration or establishment of the largest steel factory, the largest leather production complex, the largest... and the largest, all of which come with significant environmental pollution, high social and labor issues, and their consequences.

These examples are not rare. With some strong and weak connections in the past, they were so visible that occasionally they would cause trouble in different corners of the world. But today, even noticing these issues is not easy, and confronting them requires much more attention and awareness. My humble suggestion is to reflect on these invisible and ugly threads.

The Nature of Information

For you to truly see when you look at something, you need to have accurate information beforehand about what you're seeing. "Information is your gateway." Without the gateway, there is no way into the interior. But the goal is not just the "interior"; the goal is to understand and grasp the inner spaces.

When you see, hear, taste, smell, or touch, you gather "information" through your senses. But this information requires "analysis," it requires reflection. The newly acquired information must be processed with what you already know, and from there it should be analyzed. You compare it with other pieces of information, combine it, and then you can see from different angles, gaining an understanding of both the inside and the outside of a reality.

Information should lead us to "science" and help us find relationships. Let's not forget, "possessions have life." They are born, grow, mature, age, and eventually die. These possessions should be used in the direction of their evolution and updating, at the peak of their maturity, at the moment of their "care."

What are your possessions?
Your body is your possession, all its parts, your knowledge, your wisdom, your vocabulary, your experiences, your beauty. And in the final analysis, your environment, nature, and the universe are

your possessions. You must learn how to interact with these possessions in ways that benefit you.

Moral Courage

It is said that lying is the root of all corruption, giving rise to evils, impurities, and decay. But I believe that the lie itself, in many cases, stems from the absence of our "moral courage."

How much courage have we incorporated into the realm of ethics, behavior, character, and actions? And to what extent have we considered courage necessary in these areas to then analyze its presence or absence? I don't know, maybe it's a misconception of the concept of courage that has been ingrained in our minds since childhood: courage is only demonstrated by jumping over a wide river or climbing a steep wall, by not being afraid of darkness or an unfamiliar shadow! Or if, as a young child, you were able to beat up a few classmates after school, then you were really brave and fearless! Truly, you were daring!! Of course, if you fought a bully, a thief, or an attacker, then you were really a hero—there's no doubt about it. It's no surprise that our legendary heroes, like Rostam, grew from such enduring beliefs.

But today, I want to offer a definition of courage that is not so commonly accepted, one that has been called 'moral courage.'

My simple understanding of moral courage is that a person who is brave in this sense can stand tall and say the word 'no' to anything or anyone, whenever they decide it's appropriate, even if they are wrong in their judgment! Because such a mistake doesn't matter, as it can later be corrected and adjusted. Who among us, or from our surroundings, has the courage to decline an invitation from a friend or acquaintance and honestly say, 'I'm not interested in your party, I have better plans,' or even more straightforwardly say, 'I don't like you'? Who is that person?

But the typical responses are like, 'I wish you had told me earlier!... Well, we've really had bad luck... I'm really stuck here...' You see! Saying 'no'—this seemingly small two-letter word—is not so simple; it takes courage. It has a scope as wide as a city, a country, a society. It can change destinies.

I see moral courage as the ability to stand in front of someone you dislike or don't respect, or even a competitor or the head of a company, and say that you disagree with a particular action of theirs that is unjust

This is also true on a larger, country-wide, and destiny-shaping scale. Not only do people comply with those in power and lack moral courage, but if you take a glance at history, you will see that time and time again, even the great leaders have fallen into this trap and become followers of the people who dislike bluntness if it's a bit painful. I'm not even willing to place all the blame on governments in this regard. The lack of moral courage and its deficiency cannot be resolved overnight, unless we start teaching our children from the beginning of their education that recklessness and bravery do not mean crossing the street between moving cars at a red light. Let's not teach them values that are the opposite of what they should be. Let's not present the traits of virtue in reverse. Let's not confuse cleverness with trickery and charlatanism.

Because it's this common definition that calls the energetic boy who manages to skip the line at the bakery 'clever,' but we fail to realize that this same boy, when he grows up, will cut in front of you at a gas station or at the toll booth with audacity, without any sense of shame. And this 'clever' child will later press the gas pedal with confidence on worn-out tires to demonstrate a new standard of fearlessness and to confirm his 'heroism.' But this same hero, when he sees a simple traffic officer, will flatter him, kiss his hand, and show so much respect, yet would not even offer a fraction of that respect to an elderly man or woman who has little left of their physical appearance but who is struggling to maintain their citizen's rights.

It doesn't matter, even among the educated and those in positions of power, this lack of courage is abundant. A country that, despite having both friends and enemies, is plagued with disorder, and nearly all of us know that the vast majority of this chaos stems from the wrong decisions of an ineffective administration in both the past and present. Has there ever been even once, just once, a person from this crowd of small and large men, from the thousands of decisions they make, decisions that shape thousands of destinies, causing industries, commerce, and our economy to deteriorate, step forward and say, 'I was wrong'?! Why all these mistakes? They always talk about past mistakes and will gladly list others' mistakes, but will they ever admit their own? Because we haven't practiced this moral courage – the one I've been repeating – we don't value it. If you and I didn't have the courage to admit our mistakes, we would have to weave a lie to cover it up, and just like a domino effect, one lie would lead to another, until, one day, it all comes to light!

I repeat, it requires practice. One must get used to it from childhood; children must be taught that if they spill the jam jar and admit their mistake without blaming others, either they will be forgiven, or their punishment will be that at least they won't be helped in cleaning up the spilled jam. With such exercises, when the child grows up, when they enter society and have developed in this way, this beautiful moral practice will become second nature, an inseparable trait of their being. And if individuals in a society become responsible one by one, the entire society will certainly become responsible, and there will no longer be a need to shift the responsibility resulting from wrong decisions or insights onto others and fool themselves into thinking they've relieved their conscience!

The Boundaries of Thought

In the end, to what tune should we dance? If you tell us that individuality, courage, ability, virtue, love, humility, generosity, and the like are essential qualities that every human being should possess, then your behavior – oh great ones – should align with these qualities as well. Or, on the other hand, come and tell us that individuality, virtue, and courage are mere formulas! There is no need for a person to possess these traits. In that case, feel free to treat us as humbly as you wish, plant seeds of fear, hatred, cynicism, and disgust in our hearts as you please.

The pain of a human lies in the fact that one of these two things has not been done to him. If either had been done, a person would have no issue. If no one had told me that I must be capable, distinguished, and courageous, I wouldn't suffer from my own weakness, inferiority, and degradation. If I stood at the bottom of a platform, I wouldn't suffer. My suffering starts from the point where, on one side, I am placed at the bottom of the platform, and on the other, I am told that I must be at the top. Generally, once "the top" of the platform is mentioned, where I am standing is "the bottom." If "the top" hadn't been mentioned, where I am standing wouldn't be considered "the bottom." Do you understand the truth of this matter? My suffering stems from comparing these two distances. The distance between "the bottom" and "the top" and my entire life is summarized in the gap between these two! My entire life is spent in the struggle, search, and activity mixed with longing, anxiety, and fear in this gap, trying to fill it!

From the very beginning of life, individuals in the environment create situations for a child in which the child becomes trapped. On one hand, they are told they must be superior to others, but on the other hand, they are made to fail in achieving this superiority. In such a situation, the child becomes truly helpless and stuck. The pressures of the environment pull the child away from these conditions, directing them towards their own mental values and thoughts, and thus they are taken by thought. To solve this helplessness, the child turns to thought for refuge. The child disconnects from the realities of life and what is happening around them, and gives themselves over to their thoughts, letting them solve the problems. In truth, the child uses thought as a problem-solving tool. They create an identity for themselves through thought—an identity that, in contrast to their actual helpless, humiliated, and powerless existence, becomes one of strength, dignity, courage, and generally, an idealized and superior self.

However, it is not the case that the child consciously and willingly turns to thought and isolates themselves within it. This is an automatic process, a natural defense mechanism that emerges from helplessness. It can be said that this is a situation imposed on the child by the harsh and unhealthy environment around them.

If you were sitting in a serene meadow where no danger threatens you, you would have the opportunity to feel everything freely and according to your own will. You would have the chance to experience the beauties of life, to feel your own existence. In such a state, you would have a fearless, carefree, natural, and free relationship with everything. But consider a situation where you find yourself in a threatening and harmful environment, such as a battleground. In such a condition, you would not have the freedom or opportunity to experience anything freely. In this scenario, you would be forced to think about everything with fear, anxiety, and distress.

You must think about how to protect yourself from the enemy's harm, how to defend yourself, or how to escape. You must think about how to attack, how to scare the enemy, how to hide, how you can outwit them. The state of our childhood has been like that of a prey caught in a trap! And in such a situation, thought automatically takes on a life-saving role for us. Thought becomes a tool for planning, a refuge we retreat into, and from within this refuge, we devise strategies. This is why we dare not step outside the confines of this mental fortress. Behind the mental barricade, we feel a sense of psychological security. They say opium is the cure for all pain, but it itself is an incurable pain! The mental barricade is the same: it is the remedy for a thousand issues, yet it is the mother of all problems!

Now, the question is: what are we afraid of that prevents us from stepping out from behind the mental fortress? And is it not the fear of the very same things that have trapped us in this mental stronghold that keeps us there?

Once we have retreated into the mental fortress, our life and direction of movement undergo a fundamental change – without us even realizing it. After we retreat into the mental stronghold and make it our refuge, our issue becomes thought itself.

The violence and disorder of our environment threw us into the stronghold of 'thought,' but after that, the very stronghold became the issue. At one point, we were walking in a desert. Suddenly, we faced a wolf, a threat. In fear of this wolf, we sought refuge behind a wall. But once behind the wall, we realized that this wall was unstable, shaky, and weak! With the slightest breeze, blow, or shift, it could crumble and fall on us. The threat we faced from this wall, due to its tangibility and its closeness to us, has caused such fear and anxiety that we haven't had a moment to relax, to think freely and calmly. We've been so preoccupied with the fear of the wall that we haven't realized how many years we've spent behind it. The fear of the wall has entangled us so much that we haven't had a chance to peek out and see if the wolf is still there or if it has left. This is exactly our situation. We have built a defensive fortress out of 'thought,' but this very fortress, because it is 'airy,' because it is weak and unstable, because its components and parts contradict each other, has kept us in such panic, anxiety, and unease that we have lost the opportunity to clearly and precisely examine everything.

The initial blows from the environment, and then the blows that have been delivered moment by moment to this fragile and trembling wall, have been so overwhelming that we haven't realized what's happening! It's as if we've suffered from severe dizziness. The initial shock from the environment pushed us behind the wall, and due to this dizziness, we never woke up to examine the situation. But if we could wake up and reassess everything, we would clearly see that our issue now is the wall itself, the mental fortress, not any external factor. The explanation of past factors is only to understand how we ended up in our current state. The state we're in now is what matters. We are currently full of fear, full of feelings of inferiority and helplessness, full of despair, failure, regret, and many other sufferings. Where do these fears, feelings of inferiority, and failures come from? Are they from the wolf, or from the fortress? Can you find any suffering or issue, aside from physiological pain, that does not arise from the mental fortress and the structure of our identity? Is it not the fortress itself that interprets one place as 'lower' and another as 'higher,' and then tells you that because you are not on top, you are a miserable, failed, and inferior person?

I believe one of the reasons we persist in holding onto this fortress is the feeling of hatred and the desire for revenge. Think back to your childhood, when you were subjected to injustice, violence, or abuse and couldn't defend yourself, when you were forced to submit. What kind of feelings did that create in you? Was it not feelings of anger and hatred? Did you not, in your mind, fantasize about some day getting revenge? The desire for revenge and hatred have clung to our minds since childhood and still persist within us. The means of this revenge is our sense of self-worth, and in my analysis, I would say we hold onto this defensive identity and personality as a weapon to strike others. Have you noticed how we constantly flaunt our values to one another? Have you noticed how, when I succeed in showing off my knowledge, I make you feel weak, ignorant, and ashamed? Why do I spend my time buried in books, gathering information, only to throw it in your face during discussions?

Why do you search in your mind to find a question and, knowing that I don't have the answer, ask it to me? Why do you take such pleasure when four people point at you and say, 'This is the famous person'? What is the source of this pleasure? Is it not because you have been able to strike one of your weapons at me? And, of course, in defense of my own values, I too engage in efforts and sophistry to prove to you that, for instance, money is more important than art, fame is more important than wealth. Is our entire life not consumed by this exchange of values? Is there any meaning to life beyond this game of values?

God, please help us, the 'captives.' Can you see how we have become prisoners of a few words? Can you see how we have remained in a state of a distorted childhood? We have made "thought" a tool of planning, a tool of cunning and trickery. Humans love words. They feel good when a hundred or a thousand people recognize them and say their name. They are pleased by one word and displeased by another; this is the essence of immaturity and underdevelopment!

In any case, the movement of the mind is filled with revenge and hatred. Thought is identical with hatred, and this hatred, along with its accompanying fear, is the cause of the blindness and obscurity of the mind. This hatred exerts such pressure on our minds that we cannot see how we have ruined our happiness and life by striving to satisfy this demonic desire. I don't know to what extent the pleasure that hatred gives us is so strong and intoxicating that we ruin our lives for it!

Of course, the hatred itself is not important to us; it is just a means—a means to create 'pleasure.' And do you know why pleasure is so important to us? Because love has died within us! Love means the passion for life, and since we are deprived of this passion, we seek pleasure as a substitute, as a replacement for the excitement and joy, to give our lives a semblance of meaning.

In my opinion, one of the reasons we stubbornly cling to intellectual identity is that it gives us a false promise of replacement. A promise that is deceptive. A person thinks that if they can create a luxurious, capable, and glittering identity through thought, perhaps this identity can replace their crushed soul and lost self-respect. In reality, they are trying to compensate for a missing essence with a verbal phenomenon. They want to patch up their human dignity with some fancy words, but alas, how different are these two!

It's like when I am hungry, and instead of eating, I write the name of a delicious dish in beautiful handwriting and paste it on my heart! When a person loses their emotional state, it's like being hungry and always feeling empty inside, and when they build a spiritual identity using words, it's as if they want to fill their stomach with words.

We have lost the state of love, humility, virtue, courage, greatness, and more than greatness. Now, we try to replace that missing content with the words 'humility,' 'love,' and so on. Unaware that words cannot take the place of that essence.

Have you noticed how no matter where we reach or what we acquire, we still feel an inner coldness and emptiness, and we keep running more and more to reach somewhere? Why? Why does the thirst remain even after drinking the seven seas? It's because we have lost the water and now drink the mirage instead. The greatness I have lost is not something that fame, recognition, or popularity can replace. Fame gives me a superficial pleasure and intoxication, mixed with anxiety and fear, but it does not replace love or the inherent joy of life. I hope we understand the truth that intellectual identity is nothing more than a collection of sweet names and words, and words cannot heal a person's pain.

I have often asked myself: Do we consider all values and devaluations as relative and conventional? Do we not believe in the existence of absolute, non-conventional values and devalues? And if value does not exist, will a person become indifferent and apathetic toward life?

I believe: First, value can be absolute and legitimate, having a transcendent, divine origin. Secondly, our discussion is not about the values or devalues themselves. The discussion is about the 'shadow' that we have created for these values or devalues, and it is from this shadow that we have built our 'self' and 'ego.'

There are two topics at hand: one is the reality itself (whether desirable or undesirable), and the other is the shadow-like perception we have of this reality, and it is these perceptions that occupy our mind as 'self.'

We have created a sense of attachment between ourselves and all the events and phenomena of life. Or, more precisely, it would be correct to say that this attachment exists between us and the shadow of those events and phenomena, not the events themselves.

The issue is that we have created a relationship of attachment or pride between ourselves and our possessions, our states of being, and our knowledge; we have driven the stakes of our possessions deep into our hearts! We have formed a mental center from our state of being, our possessions, and our knowledge, and we have seated it as 'self' at the throne of our existence. And it is this center that governs us. In other words, a certain image governs us, and we have clung to these images with a kind of attachment that has enslaved us.

I am not saying that we should be indifferent and apathetic toward the matters of life. I am saying that we should not create a 'value-based attachment' between ourselves and these matters – an attachment that forms the foundation of the 'self' and from which the 'self' arises. Everything I am saying is about these attachments.

Not about realities, nor about the true or unrealizable qualities and meanings of humans.

Let's look at it from another window: Every day, we face dozens of problems that we don't know how to deal with. Why do you think we are not united in our relationship with life? Why is it that one part of our being is constantly at odds with another, one part condemns and criticizes the other?! All of this is because of values – values that do not stem from our nature. Had they come from there, we would not be in such conflict with ourselves.

A person's actions might seem unworthy to one observer, but to another, or according to their own criteria, these same actions might seem very humane and logical.

Now, which of these interpretations comes from the nature of human beings? The action performed is one action, but the interpretation of it is multiple or even contradictory. One may interpret it as 'unworthy,' while another may interpret it as 'noble and self-sacrificing.' And in every step of our real lives, we face such conflicting interpretations – contradictions that lead us to feelings of shame, self-blame, and dissatisfaction with ourselves. So, what is our duty?

Is the desire to help part of human nature? Yes, it's accepted! But the issue is that our help (or their help) does not stem from our innate desire. Had it come from there, we would not think of the opposite interpretation, i.e., 'unworthy.' Instead, we would be fully drawn by our nature, without caring about any other interpretation. The pain is that the basis of our actions lies in conventional values. It is these conventional values that keep the human existence shaky and unstable, plunging us into uncertainty and confusion.

My view is that if we rid our minds of these superficial values, we will return to our pure and clear nature, and this nature will govern our being and our actions, not the contradictory interpretations of others.

Passing Beyond Fruitless Thoughts

Do you agree that human energy is limited, and therefore, we shouldn't waste it? Do you also agree that the majority of human energy is consumed through thinking? Physiologists (I read somewhere) say the brain is the largest source of energy production and storage, and thinking is its greatest consumer. Keep in mind that the brain is a vast and complex phenomenon with various activities, and one of its most important activities is thinking (I'm not talking about its source of production, as that doesn't prove anything to us!). I want to focus on energy consumption.

The question is, does this consuming organ use the energy the brain provides it properly and efficiently, or does it waste it? I'm not saying thinking should consume less energy—thinking can use as much energy as it needs. What I'm saying is that it shouldn't waste energy or use more than necessary. Thought has a function in our being, and in order to fulfill its function, it must consume a share of energy. But why should it use more than its share? Is energy not a gift from God? Is it worth less than a grain of wheat or less valuable than money? Why should we let our thoughts wander aimlessly, wasting energy?

We are so attached to our sense of self and value that every question that arises in our mind is a value-based question, revolving around how to achieve worth. Instead of focusing on new, fundamental life questions, we keep thinking about where 'characters' are bought, where social success is distributed, etc.

What does energy have to do with all of this?!

Our thoughts have dominated us, taken away our control, and led us in the pursuit of 'self-worth.' We are strangely trapped by our own thoughts. What I want to say is that instead of letting our thoughts lead us wherever they wish, we should lead them. My point is that we should avoid 'fruitless thinking' and train our minds to do so. Think as much as necessary, but avoid unnecessary and pointless thinking.

One day, pay attention to your own thought processes and see what your thoughts are doing to you, what trivial matters they preoccupy themselves with.

Twenty years ago, you insulted me, slapped my face, ignored me. Well, how many times should my mind replay your insult since then? Ten times? A hundred times? My mind has repeated your insult thousands of times since then—just like a gramophone needle getting stuck on a record, repeating the same song over and over again. The needle of my thoughts has been stuck on your insult for twenty years, repeating it thousands of times.

Or to put it more precisely, since that day, my mind has recorded your slap as an insult, as evidence of my weakness, helplessness, and inadequacy. Your image of insulting me and my sense of inadequacy have stuck to my mind like a black clot of blood or a cancerous tumor, and it has 'always' been with me. It's not like sometimes it's there and sometimes it's not; the file of your insult is archived in my memory, and I refer to it on various occasions. Even when I don't refer to it, I still feel its presence in a corner of my mind. I always sense the weight of these countless files of insult and inadequacy.

Is this not a significant problem?

Oh God, if we don't see the weight and numbness caused by this as a problem, then what do we consider to be a problem?

God, help us understand the trap we've fallen into!

How thoughts torture our brain and never let us rest. The example mentioned is just one case; it's not that simple—thousands of issues—literally thousands—like the issue of being slapped, are archived in our memory, and throughout our lives, we think about them again and again, taking actions in response. The issue isn't just that we think about these matters and waste energy; images, once stored in the mind, begin to multiply and grow in complexity. Each image gives rise to side effects—such as fear, anxiety, hatred, various forms of escape, defense mechanisms, justifications, escaping from reality, delusions, ignorance in an attempt to avoid harsh truths, pessimism, doubt, contradictions, and hundreds of other issues. This is when our psychological structure becomes like a tangled ball of yarn, knotted from all directions.

Let's not misinterpret this! I'm just saying: don't waste your thoughts! In relation to yourself, others, and life's issues, any behavior or reaction that you deem appropriate is fine, but finish the issue. Don't let your brain become the nest of thousands of small thoughts! Our brains have become like those junk boxes—common in many households—where anyone throws any piece of trash they find and moves on! Our brains have become a "junk box of thoughts!" And we are unaware of how these thoughts are consuming and torturing our soul and spirit.

Thoughts, in the true sense, trample our soul and spirit. Thoughts that are fixated on the trivialities of 'self' stagnate. Thoughts that have turned these trivialities into idols and keep revolving around them! Such thoughts essentially recognize nothing but "themselves" and their own smallness!

Some people solve this issue by filling their minds with the remembrance of God, but how can our minds, filled with so much impurity—the impurity of the wicked soul—be a place for God? A mind that moves only within the confines of "self," never straying from "self," how can it grasp the boundless greatness of God? How can it perceive something beyond itself?

I think that if we empty our minds of the smallness and impurities that form "the self" and the "I" in our thoughts, we will then experience greatness and purity.

By the way, have you ever thought that if these pointless thoughts didn't exist, the "I" wouldn't exist either?

The truth is that we are enslaved by these superfluous thoughts, and escaping them is very difficult. Now, the question is, what path do we have to free ourselves from the clutches of "thought"? I think our problem isn't the "way," it's the lack of seriousness. Our problem is that we don't understand the gravity of the issue. If we reach the level of understanding the gravity of this problem, we will truly want to free ourselves from the captivity of "I," and then the way will present itself. Or, more precisely, understanding the gravity of the issue is the "way," and even the end of the path!

Let me explain with an analogy: from childhood, we are given an object and repeatedly told that it's a precious gem, and we must protect it. We hold on to it tightly, spending our entire lives polishing and adorning this fake jewel. Now, someone tells us that this object we've been holding as a jewel is not a jewel at all, it has no value, and the substance it releases poisons our blood and pollutes our entire being. All our pains, fears, sensitivities, insecurities, hatreds, and futile pursuits stem from this "jewel" and its effects.

We hear this with disbelief. The long habit of holding onto it prevents us from calmly and carefully examining it. But if we take the time, with patience and insight, to look at this object and see how it poisons us, discarding it will not be difficult. The problem arises when we haven't yet sensed the severity of the issue.

Non-being and Being

In mysticism, and especially in the mysticism of Rumi, there is a spiritual state or quality called "Non-being" or "nothingness." Rumi, in various places in the Masnavi, uses different words and forms to discuss this spiritual state and the necessity of achieving it. He emphasizes repeatedly the importance of leading a person into that state. If you've noticed, it could be said that one of the most important principles presented in the Masnavi is the concept of "Non-being" and how to achieve it. But what exactly is "Non-being"? Why do mystics insist so much on the necessity of this state? How does one transition from "Non-being" to "Being"? What is it in "Being" that is absent in "Non-being"?

When we discuss the abandonment of the "self" and reaching "Non-being," the first scary thought that comes to mind is the fear of emptiness and void. Some ask: If we lose our personal identity, what do we gain in its place? So, does "Non-being" mean emptiness and void? Does the human identity, after death, remain only as a body with some veins, hands, blood, and bones, devoid of any meaning? Does spirituality only consist of some descriptions and verbal expressions? If a person removes these descriptions from themselves, will they fall into emptiness and void? Does "Non-being" mean "nothingness"?

No, "Non-being" does not mean "nothingness." It only means "nothingness" in relation to thought and from the perspective of thought. Therefore, in that spirituality, what exists is only something that, because it is beyond the realm of thought, and thought cannot attach any description to it, is referred to as having the aspect of "Non-being"—meaning Non-being in relation to thought, not Non-being as in void or nothingness.

When Rumi says, "Lovers have set up camp in Non-being," it means that in Non-being, love exists. When he says, "O life, lovers exist in death," he means that in death and Non-being, "life" exists. But my point is not to discuss what this state of Non-being is or whether it has any benefits or not. My point is that I say the essence of human existence is in "Non-being"!

The true state of the human soul is in Non-being, and "Being" is something that has later been imposed upon it. Therefore, a person who is in the realm of "Being" has lost their humanity. Of course, sometimes we use words that are not very precise. For example, when we speak of the state of Non-being or essence, we may say, "lost essence" or "crushed spirit." These expressions, in my opinion, are not an accurate representation of the topic. Non-being or essence is not something that is lost or crushed. Let's look at the matter this way: After the mind became familiar with comparison and possession, it began to describe life. These descriptions themselves form "Being." And this "Being," whose mental activity is based on descriptions, covers the Non-being like dust. That is, the issue of "Being" is the constant preoccupation of thought, which prevents the manifestation of the state of "Non-being." Therefore, "Non-being" has not disappeared from our existence, nor has it been lost or crushed. It's enough for the mind to cease its descriptive activity for the human being to naturally return to the quality of "Non-being."

In both Western and Persian languages, there is a word called "essence." Essence means the core, essence, extract, or quintessence of something. We say "the essence of a flower," "the essence of lemon," or "the essence of orange." When you boil a flower, filter it, and throw away the residues, the essence remains. That is, the pure and concentrated part remains, the part from which the fragrance of the flower emanates.

Our spiritual essence is also "the self" minus its descriptions!

Our spirituality is the essence that remains after the attributes are discarded. It is the pure essence that has passed through a filter, and if you ask what that essence is, I would say, I do not know. Because "knowing" is the work of thought and description, whereas the essence is beyond thought and description. In any case, after thought takes control over our existence, not only does it deprive us of our essence, but it also undergoes a destructive and disastrous transformation. If thought stayed within the limits of its purpose and function, it would have properties that were entirely different from what it currently has.

The existential structure of the human being, in its natural state—that is, in the state of Non-being and without description—

has a kind of collaboration and harmony among all its parts and elements. Thought serves spirituality, not stands in opposition to it. But after that destructive change, the way it functions also changes. Inevitably, these parts act against each other and result in a breakdown of order and harmony. It's as if the tuning of the human being is disrupted, and the music and rhythm of their life become dissonant and chaotic.

The most important manifestation of this conflict and disharmony is the contradiction between love and hatred. The state of "Non-being" is the state of love, and "Being" is the embodiment of hatred! In my view, the philosophy and goal behind the formation of "Being" necessarily involve hatred and hostility. "Being" or "thought" is a tangle of hatred. What is the role of thought in our existence? Isn't it that it sits in the throne of authority and continuously weaves scheming plans? Isn't it constantly engaged in creating hatred? Doesn't it constantly think of grandeur, only to use that greatness to strike others down?

Does This Thought Movement Leave Room for Love? Doesn't this movement of thought, with such goals and intentions, leave no space for love? Doesn't it take away the opportunity for love to express itself and manifest?

Let's not take this lightly! I don't know if we fully understand the depth and severity of this process. From childhood, we have been "tuned" to the line of "greatness," set on the path of "personality," and pushed into motion. Therefore, we now think only of greatness, and even when we think of something else, we want to use it to serve our greatness. We are enchanted by glory and greatness. As a result, we are unaware of the fundamental issues of life. Our only pain is that we are not great. When someone talks to us about love, we might listen superficially, but our inner focus is elsewhere. Our inner self says, "Don't weave the literature of love for me, where's the greatness?" We truly don't feel the loss of love and what it does to us. Love has died within us, and now, with the empty grandeur of words, we seek to revive our dead souls.

Self-Confidence and the Search for Desire

My self-confidence tells me: "You will achieve whatever you desire." But the problem is, "I don't know what I want!"

These days, I am making a concerted effort to discover what I want. This has become the main issue of my life, and I think it is the main issue of human beings today. If everything about us were to be questioned, the first thing to determine would be "what do we want?" Desires are collective, individual, lasting, fleeting, rootless, rooted, whatever they are, they are decisive, foundational, expressive of personality, a sign of identity, insight, worldview, power, stability, and foresight.

A great desire is a sign of a great human, and a person reaches a point where all their desires, which are sometimes called goals, become passing gateways. They move toward the infinite. They know what they want, and what they want is boundless—for today, tomorrow, for themselves and for their growth, for their world, with no limits, ceilings, stopping points, or ends.

"Death" also becomes one of these passing gateways for them. Death is not an end; it is the beginning of the greatest influence and permanence.

And as we see more, know more, and think more, we become more cautious in choosing our goals, path, and method. This caution is not from doubt (because the soul becomes lifeless), but from research, which gives you the ability to see, hear, smell, and taste, and as you know more, you feel more secure, trust yourself more, and stand more powerfully. But now, you no longer give out advice haphazardly—without theoretical and practical validation—for anyone. Especially when people accept you, your responsibility becomes several times greater. If all the people sit and wait for you to tell them what to do, if your words become a guiding principle for others, if every small movement of yours becomes a model of behavior for those who admire and support you, then you cannot just say whatever comes to your mind—without it being accepted both theoretically and practically. Then, you become the prophet and manifestation of a culture.

Our Continuous Search

And we have tried and continue to try, we have read and keep reading, we have asked and keep asking, we have thought and keep thinking to discover what we should desire!

We question everything – all that we have and all that we are. Impartially and fairly, like researchers, we ask ourselves how what we have and what we are helps to purify life, how it enables us to stand on our own feet, how it removes depression, hopelessness, doubt, and confusion from our lives, how much it brings our hearts closer together, and where it leads us! When you discover who you should be, it automatically becomes clear what you should have. And we consider "having" to be in the service of "being." "Who" you are is the first question; "What" you have may never be the question. If it becomes clear "who" you are, if we think about "being," if we think about the positions we need to conquer, if we don't just want to engage in empty talk and fantasies, if we want to realize our theories in practice, if we want... then we must learn how to turn our words into actions, how to conquer our predetermined positions.

The path we walk is our entire life—the path that tells all contemporaries and future generations which way to go.

The beauty of your life is not in what you have achieved, but in the path you have traveled.

Ah, what a delusion! We thought life was a docile bride, sitting calmly, waiting for us to adorn her however we wanted. But we realized that life is a roaring river, endlessly moving, flowing forward until it reaches the sea and never returning to its past pathways. It visits everyone, knocks on every door, gives equal opportunities to all—but never waits for anyone. If you recognize the opportunity and seize it in that moment, you grow, you become stronger, you gain control, and you prepare yourself for future opportunities. Otherwise, you are left behind, regretfully gazing at the past.

Recognizing opportunities is the first condition. It is necessary, but sufficient only if paired with wise, timely, and appropriate use of the opportunity. Opportunities are not the same, they do not repeat, and they do not return—if you seize the first one, the second will come on its own and complement it. Someone who sees and understands opportunities well but is not agile enough to seize and utilize them at the right time will carry a greater burden of regret than someone who does not recognize opportunities or distinguish the appropriate ones from the inappropriate. And someone who does not know how to benefit from opportunities and constantly delays action will easily prioritize trivial matters over seizing the moment. When they see the opportunities have slipped away, they feel not regret but disgust—disgust with the swift and unstoppable flow of life.

Sometimes, later on, a person realizes the right way to deal with the past; in such cases, their sorrow is justified. If someone knew what to do in the moment, had the ability to act, but did nothing—the burden of "self-blame" they carry in their heart and voice becomes heavier and heavier. This "self-blame" grows over time.

There are people who have a long list of things they should do in their minds and only a short list of things they have done.

And there are people who think more about what they haven't done than what they have, carrying the weight of "what didn't happen," even though perhaps they didn't have the ability, energy, or opportunity to do more.

Aware and alert people, those who are quick-witted and perceptive, suffer more if they see, understand, and know—but fail to act. If they lack the courage to act or are prone to procrastination, they end up buying fresh bread but eating stale bread. Phrases like "putting it off until tomorrow," "later," or "now" can be both good and bad.

Someone once said, "Time itself solves many things." This is true, but only in certain situations: when a person does not know what to do, when they are undecided between two or more options, when they lack accurate information, when resources are not available, when they cannot see the next step clearly, when they are not attached to the outcomes, when they are angry, or when they feel defeated. If they cannot see the future clearly, do not recognize their own strength, and are not prepared to confront the situation, then it is better to postpone action for further study, reflection, or consultation.

People have two main attitudes toward opportunities—some are motivated by financial and material gain and are willing to do anything to obtain it. They seize every opportunity, sacrificing "being" for "having," to the extent that they trample human values in their pursuit of wealth or position.

Others are unwilling to "achieve" at any cost because for them, the "journey" and "the way" matter more than the destination. These are the ones who recognize opportunities, prioritize "being" over "having," and see work as part of their human identity.

These days, I do not understand why people question the value of "working." Even I am often warned against working too much! They do not realize that my identity, my very essence, is connected to the work I do—not because it leads to "having," but because if it were about that, I would know how to acquire more and more.

Rising individuals are unwilling to do any kind of work just to "acquire" something, nor are they willing to pursue any path just to reach their goal. Their desires and actions are aligned, their minds, words, and deeds are consistent.

If the "criteria" for growth are our influence, our ability to bring about transformation, our new ideas, and our innovative work, then our judgment about ourselves will be different. We will view our past from a higher perspective: if we are only looking back at our past achievements and taking pride in them, then growth has stopped, and only "pride" remains.

When we begin to speak, our words often flow with mentions of the "past" and the victories left behind. But if we speak of the present in such a way that it makes the past seem insignificant, it shows that we are still moving upward, because "human growth does not diminish with the passage of time."

The one who prioritizes "being" over "having," and understands that "having" serves "being," knows that our possessions can be taken from us, but our "self" cannot be taken away. It is this "self" that determines how to utilize what we have—it even chooses what we should possess in the first place.

There are people who recognize their needs, see opportunities, and find themselves released onto the field of possibilities by their awakened luck—opportunities big and small, near and far, significant and trivial.

Yet, despite their talent and energy, they engage only with the opportunities closest at hand. They see the distant horizons, but occupy themselves with the small scraps around them—their hearts are with grand treasures, but their hands are busy with mere fragments.

Everything they do turns out well; everything is satisfactory, but within the limited radius of their immediate surroundings. These people excel in their jobs, personal lives, friendships, in dispelling sorrows, in creating beauty, and in helping others. Yet their vision, capability, and insight are worthy of seizing far greater stars—capable of driving major transformations.

There are also people who enjoy blaming others—they search for reasons for their failures in someone else, or they attribute their shortcomings to others. Their negligence has prevented them from seizing opportunities, or perhaps they failed to even notice the opportunity until it had passed. Then they look around to find someone to hold accountable for what has been lost.

Is it just fine that I am the way I am?!
With each passing day, you feel closer to "it"—gradually, you begin to open up to "it" and share the secrets of your heart.

At first, you start with generalities, speaking to "it" about your beliefs, your convictions, and the principles you hold dear. "It" acknowledges and affirms everything you say. "It" validates your thoughts and accepts your truths.

You feel reassured. You think, "What I adhere to, what I believe to be true, is indeed the right path." You decide to lay before "it" the same path you have embraced for yourself.

But suddenly, "it" opposes you.

When it comes to specifics—when it comes to the actions of "it," its small, detailed movements—it responds with a single sentence, a few words that silence you completely.

"It" says, "Is it just fine that I am the way I am?"

The closer you grow to "it," the more you feel a sense of unity. The more the distance between you shrinks, the more candid and direct you become. But with that single sentence, "it" pushes you away.

It drives you back to those days when you kept your thoughts to yourself. The longer you held them in, the heavier your heart grew. And as your heart grew heavier, your steps toward "it" slowed.

But why did "it" do this?

We all have the capacity to be like "it." Because the traits that have formed, matured, and become ingrained within us shape our character.

The more we insist on clinging to our own convictions in our relationships—whether as parent and child, spouses, or friends—and the more we resist changing our beliefs when faced with the need for compromise, the more our steps falter and slow.

Let us hope that your steps toward "it" never slow so much that you lose the ability to truly understand one another.

On Women's Rights

Instead of asking, What are a woman's rights? ask, What does she aspire to? What are her dreams, her strengths, her passions, her choices? What does she hope for herself? What does she seek from life?

Let us not define women by expectations—not by what "men" want from them, not by what "society" demands of them. Instead, let us see them as individuals, as beings who grow, who create, who redefine their paths.

The pursuit of women's rights is not a distraction—it is the foundation for understanding her, for nurturing her growth, for creating a world where her talents, her ambitions, and her voice are not constrained by the boundaries of tradition. Let us move beyond dividing lines and categories. Erase the chalk marks of who "should" be what. A woman's identity is not a question of what society assigns her It is her own—an evolving tapestry of experience, instinct, and choice. Empower her to embrace all that makes her strong, to foster harmony not through submission, but through shared purpose with others. Let her flourish in what she can be—not as a complement to a man, but as a force unto herself.

Life is richer when all voices are heard, when individuality is celebrated, when the energy of one fuels the growth of all. We don't need to ask, What does it mean to be a woman? Instead, let us ask, How do we create a world where every woman can simply be herself?

To truly honor women, we must value their thoughts, their freedom, their power. Because, ultimately, greatness is not defined by roles, but by the strength of ideas and the courage to live them.

Contradiction

Does not exist! Nothing is the opposite of something else—everything is a complement. Everything is both good and bad; what proves ineffective in one context may work well in another. Anything, when justified with any description, exists on a spectrum and in a hierarchy. From the lowest degree of darkness to the highest degree of light, there are countless gradations. Darkness is not the opposite of light—without darkness, light would not exist, and light would have no meaning. Neither is bitterness bad, nor sweetness good—what tastes bitter to you may taste sweet to someone else; what destroys you may be the source of someone else's life.

We recognize everything not by its opposite, but by its difference. The masculine complements the feminine, scent complements taste, and taste complements the whole body's needs. Low is not the opposite of high; opposites do not exist. What exists is simply difference. Our standards and scales, our senses and receptors, our preconceived notions, shape us into molds, but these molds themselves are not shaped. And in our imagination, we classify, rank, and categorize even what does not fit within these boundaries. Nothing remains exactly where it is, nor appears in all its characteristics.

Images, Definitions, and Realizations Disrupt Each Other.

Every new thing is the old thing of another, and every old thing is the beginning of a new. Death and life are cyclical and revolving—what was new has become old, and what was old is becoming new! And we recognize everything not by itself, but by its difference. Without differences, existence would not be. I have always said, to preserve the freshness of life for yourself, to make the moments' vibrancy last, instead of focusing on what we lack and lamenting what we don't have, we should look at what we have and take pride in it.

But... we must not become captives of our possessions—captives of our knowledge, our open minds, our capable bodies, our beliefs and achievements, our wealth, our status, our spouses, and children. And worst of all, captives of our habits.

Let us not become captives of our possessions. We must hold them, and rule through our gains, not let them rule over us. Without possessions, we have nothing, but with possessions, we gain two personalities: the what is in the service of the who, for who matters. Use the whats to shape the who. The what is what can be taken from you, bought, or rented. But the who is you yourself—when the who is perfected, the what gains meaning. The who is what works, it holds value, it is precious, and worthy of praise.

A person is summarized in their actions.

You don't need to speak; even in the way you look, the way you walk, and the things you touch, there are signs of your spirit. They reflect the beauty or ugliness within you, they show your purity or your complexity and filth. Of course, you must speak; you must have a way to channel the flowing streams of thought and feeling.

Just as love is learned, cultivated, and nurtured, speaking—and speaking well—is something that must be learned and cultivated. It's not enough just to love, to feel tenderness, to have your heart beat for another; you must have a way to express those thoughts and feelings. Speech is the best medium, of course, if a person knows what they're saying and has learned how to say it. But you must know that your speech must be your own. It must flow from within, it must reflect your entire being. It is the inner self that reveals its treasures. Your art, your effort, your skill, and your power lie in how you present them. Have you spoken something new? Unraveled a knot? Softened a heart? Changed a path? Expressed a delicate feeling? This is what requires work—practice, learning, application, and refinement. You must value yourself, focus on your strengths and beauties, and, honestly, steer your own life, be the captain of it. You don't need to pretend to be something you're not. You must reflect exactly who you are, but you must always be vigilant about who you are—constantly maintaining, cleaning, and updating it. Don't be fooled by outer beauty, youth, talent, or today's abilities. You must work on all of these to prevent them from tarnishing and—God forbid—transforming into their opposite. Inner beauty oozes out from within. The law of osmosis applies, but I've never seen outer beauty seep into the inner self. I love outer beauty, I'm fascinated by it, but it is the inner beauty that gives meaning to it, that makes it attractive. Otherwise, that outer beauty can distance itself. A beautiful body, a beautiful face—they are among the most enchanting creations in the world. There is nothing more captivating to a person than these—they hypnotize, captivate, and make us fall in love. But all of this depends on the warmth within. It depends on culture and character—it depends on the expression of the truths you know and how you present them. There's no color more captivating than sincerity and honesty. Inner beauty is inherent, it's inherited, but like a beautiful garden, it requires care.

Our response is our culture.

"Tradition is also a part of culture, and culture is part of the grand movement and development." We have started from the first station, and we cannot approach it from the opposite direction. The more we are exposed to cultural stimuli, the more susceptible we are to them. The important thing is the response to the stimulus—evolution is just that. If there is no stimulus, there can be no response. Our knowledge, understanding, wisdom, and realism help us recognize and choose the stimuli and also shape our responses. Guidance—the stimulus and response—must align with a worldview.

A worldview must be rooted in scientific understanding.

Two people do not share the same culture, just as two people do not have the same "fingerprint." Culture is influenced by class, but class is not the only factor in defining cultural identity. Climatic conditions are also a starting point for the formation of culture, but they are only one factor. We are practicing democracy—we are increasing our capacities. We are expanding our awareness of what exists. We are questioning our beliefs and accepting what we believe, and we are practicing how to act.

We cannot eliminate differences, but the beauty, value, and grandeur of a culture lies in the harmony of these differences. Differences in age, in talent and ability, in environment and profession, in "works" and outcomes, and more. A classless society cannot exist. In the universe—as a whole—everything that exists is connected, everything influences and is influenced. The Earth follows the same laws of influence and being influenced. The creatures on it follow these rules, and humans do as well, including traditions. Human culture follows this too.

The more we are exposed to stimuli, the more responses we will have. The wise human work on Earth is to choose the stimuli and adjust the correct response.

Who is teaching you? The previous generation. To whom do you want to pass it on? The next generation. So you are a bridge between the past and the future—the "bridge of transformation!" We must take what we have, the achievements that have evolved, and work on them—scientific work, artistic work, philosophical work. Make it more beautiful, make it more fruitful, make it more effective, and make it stronger.

Ultimately, how do you view your past?
The things you did in the past—don't do them anymore, first

because your understanding has grown, and second, because those actions were responses to the needs of yesterday.

Today, needs have changed. The methods and approaches have changed, our possessions have increased, and the spaces and possibilities have evolved.

So, what should you do?

First, constantly question your desires, question your possessions, the results obtained, and the way you utilize them. Redefine everything for what it is.

Everything we have comes from the past, from our ancestors. The domain is the domain of the past, the sovereignty is the sovereignty of the past, but the future is different from the past. We do not come for the past; we want the past to build the future.

A person without a past is without identity.

But a person who has not prepared themselves for the future has no right to life. Struggling with problems gives a person the power to resist, the patience and endurance, hope, and resilience, and strengthens their thoughts.

Provided they think and struggle, question, and have an open ear for both the opposing and agreeing voices. They should be able to form a true image of themselves and their strengths and have a clear image of the problem.

"And if in love, they let their emotions lead them, in battle, they must dominate their emotions with their thoughts."

In love, our feelings should be as vast as the universe itself, and in solving problems, our thoughts should be of the same magnitude.

"Feeling," whether good or bad, positive or negative, hinders precise and rational thinking—because you place "desire" instead of "truth." You, instead of logically aligning the image of reality, glue them together according to your desire, and this results in fantasy, illusion.

We like in our love to let the scope of our imagination reach as far as it can.

It should soften our love, make it dreamy, and let us enjoy the pleasure of wandering in the world of affection.

However, when dealing with issues, solving problems, and logically navigating life, we must distance ourselves from imagination and speculation.

We must strive to get an accurate image of reality, and relate our images scientifically, logically, and based on our experiences.

In research, the researcher must not have a "desire." They must seek the truth with impartiality, without bias. Of course, "reality" is what it is, and our perception of it is just an interpretation of reality. Since we perceive "reality" with our senses, convey it to our thoughts, and recognize it with our knowledge, we must accept that we never capture it exactly as it is.

Still, blessed are those who capture clearer images, who take more reliable signs from reality, and get closer and closer to it.

The objective world is the world of realities; it is our subjective world that has a correct or incorrect interpretation of that objective world.

Change

If you want change in your environment, in those around you, in relationships and interactions—you must change yourself. Once you change, everything around you and in connection with you will change.

Change is an inner feeling that is reflected outwardly. You must change in your feelings, thoughts, and beliefs.

And this change must be carefully watched. If you accept something in thought but not in action, your personality splits—one part you accept and sometimes verbalize, the other part flows into old habits and patterns that you wish to escape from.

You must welcome encounters, encourage them, because you must create happiness in others.

To create happiness in others, you must have happiness yourself, and this is in your hands.

Creating happiness should start from the center of your life and, as you expand this radius, it will reach your family, coworkers, friends, and acquaintances.

You must always fan the flame within yourself—the flame of love and care—so that its warmth and light spread further and further. A sad person spreads the ashes of sorrow onto others. A lively and passionate person, with the rain of freshness and cheer, washes away the tarnish from the beauty of life.

Reality has a face. It has an inside and an outside—its colorfulness and diversity, its ugliness and beauty, its pleasantness and unpleasantness, depend on your perspective and the way you engage with that reality.

We must follow the path of logic and justice and pursue what ensures a future of happiness.

One cannot shape life with feelings and words alone.

Those around you may, without logic, follow emotional paths without necessary awareness. We do not revisit paths that have not provided the desired results and have led to failure. We make our expectations clear, straightforward, and unwavering, and we act accordingly. What is referred to as disagreement is, in fact, "difference." "Difference is a part of existence." We cannot remove differences, nor should we.

If we remove differences, life becomes colorless and cold. The beauty of life lies in harmonizing these differences—where differences complement each other. If a person can understand, accept, and learn how to deal with differences—adjusting their behavior according to the age, gender, education, interests, and culture of the other person they are dealing with—"at no point" will "understanding" lead to "misunderstanding."

Misunderstanding arises from a lack of comprehension. We must have the ability to understand differences and the humility to accept reality.

No one should expect everything to be according to their wishes, because nature and the passage of life make their wishes differ from others.

But they have the right, and must, always present their desires clearly, neatly, and free from superiority or self-destruction, and present their speech and actions as the peak of their offerings.

And where differences in perspective and the way of using what we have arise—let us sit down for a dialogue, to reconsider and find another way, another method, to harmonize with each other.

We aim to create pleasant and passionate spaces in life, to explore new paths of joy and happiness through consultation and empathy, and to practice independence in solidarity by sharing responsibilities.

The beauty of life lies in the harmony of differences...

Part Three
Laments in the Ruins of Time

Introduction

The year 2020 began in Iran with eerily deserted streets, an almost apocalyptic atmosphere, and the grim, fearful faces of people confined to quarantine. People stood behind windows, gazing out, recalling memories of spring's arrival not long ago, searching for a sky that was blue and hopeful. Yet the news poured in relentlessly, from every direction, with mounting numbers of the dead and infected by a strange and newly emerged virus. Ears were filled with a cacophony of rumors, or as the foreigners call them: fake news.

People withdrew into themselves, sitting on their tired and aging balconies, counting the days of despondency. Corona, this biological phenomenon, had brought everything to a halt, even extinguishing the lights in homes one by one. All the sorrows of myth and legend seemed to descend upon humanity—myself included—and they spilled, unbidden, from the tip of my pen during the endless quarantines.

What follows is the tale of two bitter, harrowing years—years of shattered hopes, trembling hands, broken keys, clenched fists, cracked voices, bent backs, and swelling griefs that weighed upon souls already scarred by a thousand wounds, their breaths growing fainter with each passing moment.

Poems

It is my fault!

O conscience; I will stay awake...
Thank you! Yesterday, you reminded me:
How much I despise roads that lead to no destination...
Windows that open to walls...
Clouds that don't rain...
And... myself! When... I don't know the destination, when I can't feel the sky...
You reminded me, I have always hated umbrellas!
Why should I make an umbrella my refuge to avoid feeling the rain?!
When the sky becomes shelter, the road is the beginning of the destination, the window is the continuation of the sky, and the cloud... the beginning of the rain...
The fault is not with the road, the window, or the cloud...
The fault is mine!
The fault is mine that I have grown old...!

Bearing the Stone

I am so tired
that I deny my existence!
And then,
I feel
my heart aches for myself...!
For myself, who so easily
gets tired!
I am scared, and I deny myself...
Without noticing the beat of my heart,
Without my eyes remembering that yesterday was the bluest day of my life,
And tomorrow may be even bluer for me...
These days, I am so tired that only the mention of his name brings me back to myself...
So that with the flickering of the first star
I kneel towards him...
I fix my gaze on the horizon
and watch the sunset with him...
After all, I've tried everything
I've even tried
to see if
my age understands my words,
I spoke from my heart to his,
from the weariness of the heart...
He gave in,
he cried...!

When the Rain Turns Away

The day when my eyes
witnessed the whisper of that Zabol man
with the cloud and the rain,
I did not know my heart
shuddered with the heart of the earth...!
With cracked lips,
with a sadness as heavy as Sistan,
it had taken hold;
Why, if you are the tear of the heavens,
do you only rain upon the fertile lands...?
Oh cloud,
this is where you should cry...
Our land is thirsty,
and the rain...
My story too,
is the tale of the anger of the rain
from the thirsty earth...!
The tale of the thirsty land of my heart,
in the anger of the friend's loyalty...
The desert of my chest
still keeps its eyes on the path...
But,
the rain does not fall...!

The Price

I remember,
I often told myself:
You are the noble person of the century!
You,
amidst all the judgments,
amidst all the enmities,
amidst all the fear,
like Moses, like Jesus,
a messenger of humanity...
A reminder of friendship, honesty...
A glimpse of divinity...!
I would say:
You are the most beautiful masterpiece of God!
You have eyes
like mirrors...
where everyone
sees light in these mirrors,
in this mirror,
the beauty of spring
and
the thousand shades of autumn are visible...
I told myself:
The flag of your wishes,
until it waves,
its budding fruits,
will be a glimpse of God's miracle...
But today, I urge myself,
sit down again and talk to yourself!

The prices shout at me:
With all this "deception of the world,"
don't fall in love again with someone who has gone...!
Don't humbly become submissive again...!

Just like the branch that, its whole life,
never bore a flower, don't be...!
Like the willow, bent down in the alley,
whose branches were broken by everyone who passed, don't be...!
I want,
on the pretext of
the little time left...
to get drunk,
to become reckless!

January 2020

Sometimes...

Today, like those other times
When I do nothing,
It passed...!
I have been taught
That life
Is made up of these "sometimes"!
And,
Sadly,
I learned
That these "sometimes"
Are taking over all of life,
Like death
Claiming it as its own...!

Ah... I wish
The good moments,
The sure heart,
The sweet smile,
The thrill of going,
Some of the loves,
Could be dried
And placed in a book
To keep and cherish...

The Manifestation of Sleep

Behind the wall of dust,
On the other side of memory,
In the air, waves of joy,
Free in the body of the wave,
The sky rejoices,
A candle fallen into the soul,
The branch of a flower,
The laughter of joy in the heart of the vase,
The alley leading
Into the embrace of hope at dusk...
Memories...
A little girl, carefree,
Dancing in my mind...
Desire... hope... tired of the cup of promises!
All the paths have been blocked for my sleep!
Sleep has fled from my eyes!

Hard Hope

In our land,
Spring,
That had not blossomed,
Withered...!
And we,
Still at the gates of destiny,
Which open "hard" before us,
We remain hard hopeful!
We,
Still,
Will not give up...
We will not step back...
We are not afraid
Of those who fear themselves...!
We
Will still wait...
We will become...
We will go...
We will reach...
We
Will laugh...!
For
I shout;
Take my hand,
Hear my heart,
Understand my words,
Here I am, alone,
Between the past and future of these roads,
Like a wandering wind,

And I seek a slope,
To find a refuge for me...
So I may become the breeze
That brings calm to the days...

March 2020

Dream

Unintentionally, I had a dream!
It reminded me
That for years, I've been seeing you in my sleep
In the sweet dreams of my childhood,
You were there
With your large, beautiful eyes,
Carefree...
In my stories
And my nightly tales,
You were always there...
I had bad dreams,
But even in those,
You were there in front of me...!
I saw you in my sleep
In the golden dreams of youth!
You were the prince of love and creation...
Now,
As the caravan of life moves on,
And there's not much of the road left to the old age destination,
Still,
Before my very eyes...
You are here...
I still see you in my sleep...
You are in my dreams...
But,
Not that deceptive dream...!
You too,
Like me,

Are torn from the distant paths,
Broken
From untangling the knots of confusion...
You too,
Like me,
Your voice,
"Alas," has become!

Familiar...

Where is that familiar one?!
The one who left in anger...!
Do you know
The world is unfamiliar to me?
Do you know
The city
Is silent, still, and blind?
Ah...! Who is the familiar one I need?
The sky, starless and moonless,
The fields and the desert,
Empty of beauty,
Before my eyes,
A world full of ugliness...
Everything I see
Is sorrow and disgrace...
There is no dew on the face of a leaf,
The vine branch
Is dry and lifeless...
The stream is dry,
Like a barren desert...
The new spring,
Like the falling leaves...
We,
Are distant from each other...
Familiar;
There is no time for complaints...
You
See for yourself;
In this spring that brings joy,

The nightingales are singing their tunes...
But the sobs are tied in throats,
Tears are still resting on lashes...
And despite all this,
I feel,
You are still familiar...
And this
Like water,
Is the essence of my life...

I am, but...

These days,
Sleep beside me
Falls into slumber!
The sun passes through the window,
The wind doesn't bring anyone's greeting,
But it knows that I am here...!
These days,
I experience
A sorrowful space,
Alone, I reflect on countless uncaptured, yet dust-covered, photographs...
Until with solitude and the love inside me,
I remain on the embankment of loyalty,
In "memory"...
These days,
I write the story of perseverance
Every day
On the mirror...
I say,
Yes, I am here,
But I am in pain...!
These days,
Anxiety waves through the air,
The air is filled with the scent of grief...
Grief upon grief!
I fear the grief of grief!

Understanding of Perception

When things get bad,
They get really good!
Everything suddenly makes sense to you,
You understand the price and value of everyone...
You realize how lonely you are!
How abandoned...
You understand that you can't ask anything from anyone!
You feel loneliness,
You understand it, you grasp it!
You reconsider all your beliefs...
Your perspective on values changes...
On prices...
On trust...
On presences...
And on absences...
These aren't bad!
When things get bad, they get really good...
You finally realize
What you've reached,
You have a true understanding,
You've grasped an understanding of the issues...
Your eyes open wide
And you see around you
Who's there
And who isn't...!

Memory

My gaze fixates
On the wall of childhood...!
The scent of green boxwood leaves
On the kindnesses and childish friendships...
On the rush to grow up!
My gaze lingers
On the flower of the carpet!
I stare
At a sorrowful image...
The face of youthful anger,
The face of the monster of ruin,
The face of a demon and darkness...
I remain fixated on a notebook,
On a poem full of pain...
My gaze groans
On the tall walls of the house,
On the green leaves of the vines...
You were a traveler...
Not in imagination,
But I know you truly left...
I know, you left in the season of the garden's nakedness!
In the season of the strange crows' migration,
At the start of the season, the fall of wandering clouds...
I knew,
I knew,
The day I remembered your departure,
I wrote a poem – not in a notebook,
But on a handkerchief,
A poppy;

The thirst in your foreign eyes will claim you...!
I knew,
I knew,
If they poured all the freedoms of the world
Into the cup of your eyes,
You'd still go on,
Wandering in the corners of walls,
In the far reaches of democracies,
You'd go and keep going,
To sing of the familiar scent of the alley...
I know,
I know,
You'll take the desired hope,
By breaking
The cross of the silence's lock,
In the season of lotuses,
To witness
The love of tangled hair...
I know,
I know...

The Scorched Heart

Silence in spring
Is like the song of a single tear,
Like the loneliness of a fleeting glance,
Like the erosion of an endless path...
It makes the night
Heavier and heavier...
Silence in spring,
Where neither the desire to see the locks of the mad willow
Is tempting,
Nor the blossoming rain of the garden...
The sun,
You will find, is subdued by the shadow of distances...
In this spring silence,
I wonder,
I am so sad, so sad, so sad...
I die from this sadness,
I die, I die, I die...

Futility

These days,
Everyone is thinking about one thing...
Or at least,
It has become the mental preoccupation of many people on this earth;
"Futility"!
No one thinks anymore
About the dawn without light,
Or the night without stars,
About the merciless and burning sun,
Or the moonlit nights
That no longer
Witness the lovers,
No one thinks about them anymore...!
Of course,
There are those who
Think about tomorrow, which is like the wildflowers in the garden,
But even they
Should think about the mechanical doll in their home...
So that whenever they wish,
They can mindlessly
Watch its repetitive movements
With love...!
Because tomorrow, too,
Is exactly like these days...!

Understanding Love

I had a mentor who spoke of love,
Of learning love,
Of learning the soul,
Of the sweet nectar
That nourishes the soul...
He even said:
"The fortune of speaking with that soul companion, is enough for us!"
And I was amazed!
I was amazed by the simple word "life"...
Because,
To me, love
Was an unsolved mystery,
A story left behind
From the souls of mankind
From the very beginning...
And perhaps
It will remain in their hearts forever...!
I
Easily freed myself
From understanding love,
Walking barefoot
In the river of life!
So
I wouldn't be left with longing!
I close my eyes,
I surrender myself to the flow of the river,
To let it
Take me wherever it may...

Love
I have spoken of it,
The weight of my gaze, truly—
In the depths of memories settled in the core of my soul...
I don't know,
Maybe it's regret...
Regret of understanding this very moment!
Life, love,
Is all my passion and desire
For tomorrow,
A tomorrow that I know,
Is full of yearnings...
Because
My vessel is full of regrets...
Life,
Is nothing but a simple custom...
A custom of welcoming fate...
A fate that none of us
Can turn away from!
They say: Life is the understanding of misunderstandings!
That we didn't understand why,
Why now,
Why here,
And why this way
We meet each other!
We didn't understand that
The sky, calmness,
Love, and being together,
Were the fine taste of our fate...
And we,
How poor we are in understanding fate.....

The Deprived of Love

These days, the weight of my thoughts
Has become the weight of unfamiliar endings...
From my tired body,
The flowers of hopelessness,
After years, have blossomed...!
My senses are filled with
The smell of your lonely flesh...
I want to let these unsaid longings pass...
I want

As always -
To have hope that,
There will always be another "good" tale left for us...!
But in these dark nights,
How can I endure the repetitive, dusty days?
Can you endure?
Can we endure?
Someone gave me hope;
A sky full of stars,
A world of days without nights,
And nights that blend with the day...
They wish this for me...
And for all those days when
We didn't hear each other's sighs of pain,
I ask the God of the heavens,
To let us rest beside each other...!
It is not right, for no one to believe my oath...

In this hot summer full of sun,
It is not right for my dreams,
Which want the garden without sorrow,
To be left in wonder...!
I now,
On the birthday of that compassionate saint,
From the pile of carpets,
Arrive at the sacred window,
To gaze upon God...
And cast Satan,
Behind the high walls of prayer,
Exile him,
Wandering in the darkness of the deprived of love...
What belief is this belief!
That the morning of hope
Is still standing firm...
In the blue sky,
With hands raised to God,
They will surely be full of flowers – and with the fragrance of flowers –
In the ebb and flow of life,
It will come...
It is not futile
That in my eyes,
You should not trust the clouds!
... They are wanderers
In the morning abode,
All seeking which flower's fragrance to love?
With certainty, I say:
I know the answer!
Follow the flight of the birds at dawn...
The miracle will happen...
And the fragrance of the acacias of the garden,
From the hill to the alley,
From dreams and memories to our room,

Will come...
And now,
You will say:
Life is no longer
The mysterious world of desires...
What belief is this belief,
That the night...
Does not last?!

April 2020

Not Reaching

In the evening,
When I think of the volume of the atmosphere;
When I gaze at the multitude of planets...
When I ponder the loneliness of emotions...
I comprehend the mountains and their deep sorrow...!
Because,
A mountain does not meet another mountain...!
And this
Is a great sorrow,
The sorrow of not reaching!
But,
I am amazed at the condition of these people...
People who reach each other,
Yet,
Their sorrow
Is no less than that of not reaching!

Hard on Ourselves

We humans,
Our hearts are empty,
And we constantly tell ourselves:
We are hard on ourselves, life is hard...
Instruments have become sorrowful,
And the days of sorrow,
Heavier each day...
What remains in our hearts,
Is sadness from the present and longing for the past,
And fear of the future...
And our hearts,
Are dark and sorrowful...
We reach the night from one another,
And flowers die with our arrival,
And trees breathe with our departure...!
With a dagger in hand and a smile on our lips,
We have regret on our tongue, hatred in our hearts, and tricks in our minds!
We do not tremble from the cold of hearts!
We humans,
Have forgotten the smile of the sun,
The song of the canary,
The greeting of a friend,
The tear of joy,
The look full of water,
And love for humanity...
And we keep telling ourselves:
We are hard on ourselves, life is hard...!
In the twilight of loneliness,

We break and do not listen to each other's cries...
We place pride like a mountain of sand in front of ourselves...
As if not even the rain of tears can soften our hearts...
We do not see how much we suffer in separation,
What we sing, what pain settles in our hearts...
We seek refuge from bitterness to bitterness,
From envy to hatred,
And from grudges to animosity...!
We speak our complaints to friends so that we do not hear their discontent!
We carry tears in solitude so that we do not understand mockery!
And we sigh...
We loudly wail so that no one hears our cries...
So that sorrow greater than what is already in our hearts does not visit our hearts...
And we laugh and say:
"We are hard on ourselves, life is hard...!"

June 2020

Savior

I dreamt,
On a broken, sail-less raft,
Dazed and powerless,
In the endless and crushing waves of time,
I cry out:
O Savior,
Come to my rescue...
From the far distance,
Beyond the countless waves,
My eyes
Encounter the shape of a form...
For a moment,
I plunge into thought,
Whispering to myself, I give hope,
He is there, my savior!
Waiting,
In the moment of meeting, I wait...
Suddenly,
A hideous, evil demon appears,
I tremble
And lose my strength...
In the surge of the wave,
A cave opens its mouth...
Filled with ivory spikes!
Relentless and merciless,
It attacks me and my raft—
Like a bird—
The storm; fierce,
The sea; terrifying,

The roar of thunder striking life,
And I,
Am born anew
In the bed of the waters,
With the final cry of my being,
I awaken from sleep!!

Creation of the Apocalypse

In this wasteland of the world's name,
Every morning and every evening,
For us, the thirsty for human love,
The hungry masses of disorder,
In this pure and weary thought of "wandering,"
Our soul, body, and spirit,
Burnt in the spell of this fading regret...
What thoughts and solutions do we have?
In these reckless games of aimless being...
In this desperate quest without destiny...
I do not know the secret of my creation.
I do not know,
From which branch of these travelers we come!
I do not know,
What is God's and Satan's share
In my existence?
But I want,
Amidst memory and regret,
Amidst the silence of my words,
Amidst the defiance of my gaze,
To be patient and persistent...
To read life, line by line,
In harmony with the growth of body and soul...
Once again!
So that no dust of silence remains
In the pages of my heart,
On the throat of my notebook...!
I want,
Even two days before my end,

With a candy flower and a branch of sugar in hand,
Before I hang my shirt
On the laundry line of this world,
To write special names
Of this "apocalypse" of "life"
In the newspaper of existence...!

The Gem of a Smile

My days pass,
And I am still in wonder...!
My nights pass,
And I remain in my solitude...!
In this dream of loneliness,
In this
Futility, the entire futility, moment by moment...
I am in search of the gem of a loving smile!
And this smile,
In the city of emotional collapse,
Is very rare...
Among these crossroads—where countless questions are asleep,
I am thinking of a mirror,
To see myself again...
To place myself in the ruthless dark road,
And in the cold, bloody cellar of a cold stare,
And in the beautiful and golden dream of the sunlight of hope and love,
To mourn the cries of the spring of life...
Oh... how I wish,
That the sun would smile soon...!

Ignorance

The trees
don't know the name of the season.
The flowers;
they don't know the days, the nights, or the hours.
But
when the sun shines,
they take life from its light
and breathe for just a day.
What we call "night,"
is simply the exhalation of that breath...!
Nature is never concerned
with the names of the seasons,
or whether the flowers know the time,
or the trees know the name of the season.
Whenever
the exhalation stretches,
whenever
the dead skin of the leaves falls,
the tree
neither blooms
nor complains about the passage of time...
What we call "winter,"
is just a seasonal sleep...

Neutral State

I am so weary and longing
of artificial flowers...!
For they are the messengers
of the garden's death in the cold of autumn...
I am so weary and longing
of artificial people...!
With their smiling lips and deceitful faces,
they go towards the spirit of kindness and generosity
and we
never understand!
Artificial affections,
how devoid of color and insignificant they are,
so cold, reproachful, and worthless...
But alas,
we never know!
I never want these cold, artificial smiles...
For I know
they are like a dangerous sting, a bringer of death...
But alas...
We are in need of a smile full of warmth,
but
we die too soon...
And this
is a pitiful, painful cycle...
And even after death,
these cold faces will weep!
And how unfortunate, for even that
will be cold and artificial tears...!

July 2020

Autumn

How quickly autumn has come again...
How quickly my music
has turned yellow...!
If we are entirely
yellow and withered,
we haven't given our hearts
to autumn...!
We have become a tree without leaves,
We ourselves
have become the season's craftsmen of sadness...!
I
complain about autumn
and find peace,
like that tree in autumn
when all its leaves have been carried away by the wind...
This autumn,
I am lonelier than autumn...!

Autumn Gaze

When autumn arrives,
there is something in the human soul,
a kind of longing,
that seems to bloom with endings...!
Autumn
is the season of reminding us of forgotten memories...
People whose summer warmth or spring freshness
have long been forgotten...
All of them hang on the branches of a frostbitten isolation,
so that as soon as your eyes meet theirs,
they let go like innocent children—waiting for attention—
onto the ground,
memories crinkling beneath the trembling, cautious steps of those who think
they understand what has been lost, but haven't...!
Although the pain of autumn,
with its unparalleled intensity,
showcases the miracle of nature with pride,
and builds grandeur from decay...
Autumn, for me,
has long been more than its poetic beauty;
I breathe in its sorrow and
longing...!
I know thinking of the poetry of autumn is not for joy or delight,
and it rightly deserves its due,
but from my perspective,
it is a surrender to lethargy and despair!
It imposes upon you the grief of "absence" and loss,

so that beneath its grand and deceitful cloak,
it accustoms you to nothingness!
Here, autumn—
at its most optimistic view—
its essence, the whispers of its scent,
all seem like a gift of a brief moment or the experience of "being alone"…!
Generally, in the solitary banquet of autumn,
a poet no longer, like spring,
thinks of rhyme and meter, and in isolation, weightlessness, and confusion,
such sorrow and melody falls
from the sadness of autumn that a person learns,
how to understand
with the blaze of autumn's fire and the pitiable sway of bare trees,
and the dizzying haze of the dim sunlight at sunset,
measuring and weighing the essence of life...
The legacy of autumn,
for me,
is the sorrowful grandeur
of the memories of those who are gone...

Autumnal Friday

Like words,
under this autumn sun,
in the boundless stillness of Friday,
sluggish and weary,
they refuse to leave my pen...
I sit waiting,
for tomorrow to arrive,
to immerse
the faded colors of my soul
in the radiance
of its hopeful eyes...!

August 2020

The Lover's Pomegranate

They say:
A fragment of eternal paradise
fell from the heavens,
shattering like a mirror upon the earth.
The mirror broke into countless shards,
each one finding its way into a person's hand.

Whoever saw their own face in the shard
was lost to ruin,
but those who glimpsed the face of their beloved
found eternal love.

They saw me wandering calmly through the alleys,
a mirror in one hand,
a pomegranate in the other,
and laughter blooming within me
like the joy of young girls.

They told me,
"Take the mirror home,
and bandage the pomegranate's wounded skin
with a white cloth."

They didn't know
I brought the mirror to the streets
to show people their true reflections,
to reveal the wounds they hide.

And I left the pomegranate untended,
its split skin open,
so lovers could see
how a pomegranate falls in love—
and how it breaks.

The Scourge of Journey

Until I rise for the journey,
No poem will I pen!

These restless days,
stooped over the lifeless airport hall,
trace my steps—
their watchful eyes
fixed upon this window.

Streetlights and the control tower,
like glowing enchanted spires,
stain the heavens
with a tarnished hue,
and virus trails
in their amber glow
mimic the pockmarks
of ancient plagues.

My hands,
overflowing with the dawn's radiance,
press firmly
against the parallel lines of the horizon,
as I drown in the song of mariners,
yearning by their feverish, rain-drenched docks
for oars they cannot grasp.

Yet I—
Until I rise for the journey,
No poem will I pen!

September 2020

The Miracle of the Rain

I confess,
I was wrong...!
The rain must be read,
Its lines of wonder,
Its blue watery letters, carrying the memories
Of distant seas...
The rain is the tear of those cast into the sea by a storm,
The ultimate joy of thirst...!
It is the hunger of a woman
Who tears her own soul
In the longing for love...!
It cannot be denied...
It cannot be ignored...
Its recurring freshness
Promises a birth of authenticity...
On whatever it falls,
A laughing voice rises within it...
With an pomegranate in hand,
I walk beneath the rain,
To blush its redness,
And smear it on the sorrowed cheeks of autumn...

Languor

I gave my evening, my dusk, my night
to a cold and callous couch,
its silence deeper than mine.
I…
made no effort to climb
out of the hollow of my loneliness.

My hand,
a ghost at my side,
wanders aimlessly—
numb, detached.
In my mind,
a faint flicker of some brighter future
warms itself in the shadows,
but the sleep of evening
has stretched far into the depths of night.

Night—
like stagnant blood,
has splattered across my face.

Awake yet dreaming,
I see:
the sun, a cancerous swelling,
bulging on the horizon.
I see:
a veil of mist
settled between me and my hands.

No matter how long sleep lingers,
it is still just sleep.

I must prepare myself
to pay the ransom of another day,
to wait—
until tomorrow's dawn
opens its heavy eyes
and looks upon me.

October 2020

Traveler of Light

I wish to close my suitcase!
I tell myself:
Let the wind
boldly shatter the ancient orbits of misfortune,
let it lift away
the intrusive presence of worries
from the window of my skull.

I wish,
from now on,
that the gifts from my ideal city
be nothing more than
the breeze of sweet memories,
the smile of peaceful satisfaction,
the dream of a rainbow in my mind—
nothing else.

I wish to fill
the gaps of working hours
with the melody of pure harmony,
to close my suitcase!
For a journey
parallel to the moonlight,
alongside
the morning release of dandelions...

I want to begin

to mend my cracked memories
with the same breeze bloomed in the dawn.
I wish...
but to see all that beauty,
I still have not found the mirror.

My suitcase in hand,
a wanderer of the world.

Resolute Hope

I summon myself with quiet force:
On the petals of dawn,
like dew, strive—
think pure, think clear…

Let the wild winds' reckless fury
scatter unheeded,
lost to the void.

By midday's golden embrace,
drink deeply
of light's crystalline streams—
a honeyed hymn from the sun's core.

So that when evening descends,
you rise like a star,
casting brilliance upon dimmed windows,
shattering shadows
with your eternal glow.

Alive in the Tomb

I searched for a trace,
To ensure I never turn back to the past…
But I found
Not a shadow around me!
I cut away my memories,
Yet saw
Nothing in my reflection!
Behind me,
A road full of waiting…
But I told myself,
"Enough of resting in hope!"
Half-dead songs,
Oh, voiceless songs…
I don't know,
I don't know why I am restless?!
I don't know why
I want to get used to this empty mirror!
But no…
I must draw a line over the voice of my wounds,
And betray even my habits!
I want
In the exile of murmurs,
To let
The silence of this lonely heart
Die…
So perhaps,
The death of my voice
Can take vengeance
On my doubts!

These Days…

These days,
I am but a passerby, bitter and forgetful…
Like a breeze
That sweeps past the bridge of shattered trust!
And from the waves of the crowd,
I gather the fleeting resemblances…
These days,
The resemblance of the departed
To the dead of millennia has grown faint…
These days,
I can only sit,
Waiting for that heavy shadow of hope,
That is on its way…
These days,
With what slowness, and what weight,
A sigh falls from my depths…
These days,
I am still dizzy with autumn,
And my gaze, wet and weary,
Scratches the horizon of dusk…
These days,
Only a single autumn-stricken tree outside my window
Comforts me…
These days,
Autumn longs
To be beside me!
These days…

Complaints from the Rain

The rain falls,
But this rain,
Has nothing but weary clichés
To offer!
And no flower, I fear,
Will escape the grip of the season's snare...
In this rain,
Only this thought of mine
Has sprouted
On the damp railings!
Ah... the rain,
How late you fell upon my shoulders...
The brightness of my eyes,
Whitened by the salty gaze of waiting nights!
The playful glances of the clouds
No longer tempt me...
The wet branches of autumn
Have sold the fragments of my being,
Full of secrets and dreams,
To the rainbow of imagination...!

December 2020

Fear of Me

Until now,
I have never shared my dreams with anyone!
Everyone thinks
That I
Am a light sleeper, with no time to dream!
Some say
I am an emotional person...
Shaking my head when I see the children on the streets...!
Yes,
Believe me,
I have no time, nor a heart for it!
I grow old even in the reflection of my own flight...
For centuries,
I have sustained myself with my dreams,
And constantly
I have starved!
If I pause,
I realize I've been forgotten...
For the smile I give
No longer resembles my own!
The laughter I carry now,
Except as a strategy,
Is nothing else!
And this,
The final arrow,
Leaves no peace for the beauty of my cheeks...
My dreams,
For years,
Have fled from me,
In fear of this monster...

Her Intent...

She said,
"I wanted to tell you of my nightly tears,
of how I wept through all the seas,
through every drop of water...
I wanted to tell you of my longing,
and the dagger of the night,
of how I sang laments and wailed,
and through all the waters,
I called for you."

Yet still, she said,
"I burned your poem entirely!
To write anew,
a verse that breathes life,
and opens through the grace of its window,
to make a friend of time itself."

She said,
"Life is no longer
a cryptic world of desires for me...
Reaching now is not
the pursuit of fleeting fortune...
No longer..."

She said,
disheveled and restless,
"I want to seek out
the shadows of those I've lost."

She said...

The Waits of the Winner

In the ruins of waiting moments,
yellow leaves scatter through the street…
The sky weeps for me,
for the barren desert of my chest.
Flowers' stems
wither in my grasp…
The night bird sings its lament,
while time's cupbearer
pours pain into my heart's chalice.

Yet until dawn,
I remain,
my eyes fixed on the dust of the road,
chased by sleeplessness.
On my lips,
a question lingers, frozen:
Why did you not come?

Ah… the tale of your silence
is like a bird's longed-for flight.
We never know,
until it arrives,
who truly wins the wait.

January 2021

The Words of a Gaze

There are words within me,
words of years gone by,
from when my poetry
was merely an excuse…
Words of a past
untouched by hopelessness,
untainted by lost dreams.

Though the dance of swirling smoke
stands between us,
though once again,
with bitter silence,
I seal my lips from confession,
still,
in our gazes,
secrets lie dormant.

In our gazes,
veiled words linger:
"With you, life is worth living.
With you, life is a mistake."

I am the gentle gazelle
of this familiar plain,
and you,
the lone shepherd of my desolate fields.

You are my kindred.
You are my solitude.

Each Night...

Always, at this hour,
I take up the pen of fate
and begin gathering memories.

Each night,
not just at this hour,
but throughout the dark,
I pass by the scent of night-blooming flowers,
indifferent.

Each night,
around this very time,
I wish for life,
just once,
to taste like something
other than hunger.

Each night,
the world, at this hour,
remains untouched,
unmoved,
by the murmurs
of a man and woman
behind the café window.

Each night, after dusk,

I look at my hands—
at all they failed to hold,
at all they could not do.

Always, at this hour,
I remember the hands
that surrendered to a cold handle.
I count those hands,
one by one,
to find my way to sleep.

Because each night,
the weight of my pain
opens no door.

The Spell of Soil

I feel it,
the soft embrace of an ambiguity,
something like the unfolding of a grass stalk,
deep within the warm soil...
I feel it,
the soil is mine alone,
and nothing else.
Alas... that all my seeking was for the river of light,
but the waves of tears are all I've gained!
Do you see me?
Sitting on a mound,
with open hands,
I surrender the earth,
in my weary palms,
seeking refuge...
But I feel it,
the darkness of life
is slowly ruining me...

If Only…

If only,
if only people
could find each other sooner…
From far-off distances,
from the depths of unrelated,
unconnected ties…
From the very place
where the artist of fate has written:
"These souls belong together!"

They would become
companions,
friends…
Kindred spirits,
sweet as life itself!
They'd find their place
on the mantelpiece of each other's hearts,
where their words
carry a gentle charm,
and their laughter
makes hearts weak.

Their very presence
would be pure,
irreplaceably sweet!

If only God
would never take
such people
away from us…

The Dance of Fate

Do you know
what tale this is?
Do you sense
what sign it holds?
And do you see
how this need of ours,
this loyalty we give,
is but a fragile balm
to the reckless fleeting of our days?

I know well
that in this grim feast of fate,
my story and the cup I hold
mirror the night and its dying flame,
a story told in laments—
of time and destiny's cruel embrace.

For we are prisoners,
chained to fate's whims,
and time itself
is the thief of what destiny owes us.

Our silenced lips
have spun too many tales,
our tear-streaked eyes
have betrayed the secrets
we swore to guard.

Do not weigh me down,
O companion of my waiting,
so I may speak
of a tale from the beginning—
of those springtimes
sweet with song,
untouched by the long shadows
of unbloomed flowers.

The Air of Geraniums

Let's breathe again,
just once more!
Perhaps this air
is laced with the scent of tuberose…
Perhaps,
somehow,
we've forgotten how to truly live…
Perhaps,
the waters are still clear, still sweet,
and we
have merely failed to ask the breeze
to recall for us
the memory of geraniums!

Those moments when light,
unrestrained,
raced through the window toward them…
I could not control the light,
and that
was a profound, sacred joy.

Perhaps,
I can once again
seek out even the grandest dreams.
But this time,
I've learned:
In the explosion of great dreams,

I must include everyone,
so that, in the coming spring,
even the street children selling fortunes
can hang the rags of their misfortune
upon the blossoming branches
of these very dreams.

I want to share these "perhapses,"
these dreams,
with everyone—
with those
who found the beauty of life
in fairytales,
who saw existence
prepared within both dreams and reality combined.

Life,
it is beautiful in these "perhapses."

February 2021

Final Part
The Passing Shadows

Fifty Years

I have turned fifty,
in a feeling saturated with regret for the days gone by;
half a century!
And despair, and fear of the days ahead…
Even a sensation, brimming with emptiness,
emptiness without urgency.
I have turned fifty—not suddenly,
but for years, I awaited its arrival!
And yet, with one lingering thrill,
a thrill born from the revelation of a feeling:
the feeling of fifty.

I begin my fiftieth year
with birthday wishes from telecom companies,
bank notifications,
and unopened life insurance messages.
This life that races on,
its spring and summer flash by,
and I mostly see autumn and winter
etched into the hollows beneath my eyes.
I run too—I run, endlessly seeking.
I run toward a "yes,"
and I run toward a "no."
I don't know…
but I want to run toward Her.

Though today,
I lie on the shore of a small sigh,
with my eyelids heavy, drooping over my weary eyes.
I have run through all fifty years,
I remember them all.
I even remember how my mother
conceived me in the month of Mehr.
Yes, I remember it all.
I have seen all my life unfold,
and I carry the sorrow of those sighs.

Oh, Life, I have seen you!
I saw you, Childhood,
you who fled from me.
I saw you, Youth,
you who grew weary of being with me.

I know…
my generation never had a childhood,
and no one ever apologized for that.
But I, I will apologize to myself.
I remember it, and I bid it farewell.
I remember so I can expand my children's childhood,
so they can live more fully,
so they can love more deeply.

Oh, Life, I have seen you.
I have seen you, the heavy burden of humanity!
I have seen you, the costly ignorance of mankind!
My pain—
it is the sharp wings of your flight!
My pain—
it is the disregard for moments spent with you.

I know,

your rights are not in the bitter words of interrogation lights.
But my rights are not the punishment
for Adam's forgetfulness.

Today, my fiftieth year demands I learn
even from the decayed planks of the sea—
it demands we take to the waters,
to fish even in muddied depths.
For that is the bolder way.

By the way, my father was named "Sadegh"—
a truth-teller among truth-tellers!
He, in my childhood,
would sit on the sun-scorched porch of our southern home,
reciting elegies in harmony with Faez:
"Oh, the heart, so heavy, so sorrowful…"
I did not understand!
What does "heavy-hearted" even mean?

He would recite Baba Taher,
about daggers of steel piercing the soul
in search of freedom.
I remember it well—
at that same time,
he too was fifty.

But he knew how to soothe a wounded arm
with the balm of sorrow and faith.
Indeed,
without faith,
what balm could heal ancient wounds?

Recklessly, in the intoxication of youthful days,
I would reopen the wounds of my own journey.

The blood that flowed in the city
turned the tragedy of friendship crimson.

Outside the window of youth,
the sun had died.
With a hundred knights of faith,
I would call upon the dead sun
to ride its coffin once more!

My eyes, my weary eyes,
still search for the flowers of my youthful garden,
those red blossoms lost amidst smoke and dust,
amid the scent of gunpowder,
amid the roar of tanks and bulldozers.

I know you still doubt me.
But this is my belief:
It was my faith
that perished beneath the wheels of death's chariots—
those crimson wheels
soaked with the blood of love-struck wanderers,
beckoning me with their flickering lights
to "Stop."

And with that "Stop,"
at twenty,
I began to "question" myself.
But now, as I reflect more deeply,
I see how much I wronged myself.

The roots of my thoughts
are stronger than time's sharp axe.
The roots of my thoughts,
heavy with branches,
know how to bloom.

With a passionate head,
they await the spring and the sun,
to pass through this garden—
the garden whose flowers are waiting.

Let us learn,
and teach,
the precious fawn of life.
For in my voice,
dozens of birds
await a song of revival.

Kish Island, June 2018

Lament

A strange sorrow brews within my chest,
Pride in my partial wisdom finds no rest.
Perhaps I nourish a rebellion untamed,
A defiance of humanity, its essence defamed.

I long to scream in this barren sphere,
Where human knowledge dwindles, unclear.
But truly, where will my cries take flight?
To what purpose burns my voice's light?

Perhaps that lone minaret in the narrow lane,
Might purchase the melody of my pain.
Or the pockmarked peddler, weary and bare,
May bid me shout his cheapened wares.

Perhaps the old shepherd on the endless plain,
Will find my voice a soothing refrain,
To lull his flock with my wandering call,
In the vast expanse where shadows fall.

Ah, even this small purpose, this fleeting grace,
Calms the storm in my heart's embrace.
But know this, for some time now,
I've grown weary of my human vow.

Of the burden of being, I've tired so deep,
Of the arrogance our nature dares to keep.
Let me live, for a while, like the sheep—
Simple and free in a dreamless sleep.

Let the height of my joy, my life's elation,
Be a green pasture's sweet salvation.
Let my stomach's delight be my grandest thrill,
As I graze in peace upon the hill.

Let me be spared from blame or sin,
As I wander to heaven with innocence within.
And perhaps, when the butcher's red-stained hand
Reaches for me, I'll take a stand—

I'll see his blade as my flag of release,
A mark of freedom, a symbol of peace.

The Locks of Jasmine

Amid the division of words,
Spread upon the table of my solitude,
I rise, lantern in hand,
To dust off the forgotten lexicon—
Of truth, of kindness,
Of friendship, and the art of love.

I set forth,
To cleanse the tarnished heart of years gone by,
To weave poetry anew,
Fragrant with the spirit of humanity.

But my Simurgh of thought,
Its wings yet unspread,
Was crushed beneath the avalanche
Of deceit,
Wrath,
Betrayal.

It fell to the ground, silenced.
Ah, woe to this human race,
Madness grieves in its wake!

Purity has faded,
The garden bereft of the jasmine's perfume,
Its blossoms burned,
No melody rises from the flute.

Ah… perhaps the windows are sealed shut?
A sorcerous dragon crouches still,
On the river of life,
Heavy with the weight of humanity's stone.

Simply Being

I long to surrender my rational days,
To nights brimming with the joy of "simply being."
This barren expanse is a world in itself,
Where no shame meets a child's poverty-stricken gaze.

Here, thought thrives, unbound by proof,
Free to roam without reason's roof.
Humanity clings to no map, no history,
Untouched by chains of pride or dignity.

It does not bend to honor's demands,
Nor build itself on character's sands.
It simply exists—steady, profound,
Bearing patience where no haste is found.

Or perhaps it does hurry, and I cannot see—
A rush to spread this vast emptiness endlessly.
Maybe that's why philosophy schools abound,
And theology's theories so richly resound.

For here, in this quiet and boundless land,
Existence carries no master's brand.
Heavy with presence, serene yet bold,
It speaks no truths, yet countless are told.

Fifty-One

Today,
Yes, today,
I've circled the sun fifty-one times!
Years and years before I could circle anything even once,
I imagined this endless spinning with such wonder and confusion.
But now,
I feel as though
The dimensions of my being
Have grown so vast, like my solitude,
That even a mighty body like the sun
Seems bewildered by the immensity of my existence.
It feels, somehow,
Lost within the vastness of my soul.

And yet I,
In complete humility,
Cherish this lost presence within me.
Even the particles of its light,
Dancing among the motes in my eyes,
Make my heart flutter with joy.
It seems,
The longing of my estranged heart
Lies within the fountain of the sun's hands.

The turning of all these days and years
Commands me
To pull myself out from the confines of words,

And to keep letting go
Of the memories that have passed.
In my moments of weariness,
I plant a few stalks of narcissus
In the fossilized seconds of my fleeting joy,
And I blow dandelions
Toward the uncertain growth of "love."

Though, like countless barren seeds before,
It blooms amidst ashes of forgotten dreams,
Rising in my heart
As if it were born alongside my own birth.

Each year,
Behind the veil of my weariness,
I stand at the grave of lost memories,
Extinguishing the candles on the cake of absence,
Of what never was.
I blow them out,
And blow again,
But will this heavy dust
Ever lift off this one particle of life?

I know,
I know, before I opened my eyes to the sky,
The sea was already striking its head against the shore.
And I know,
Before I began,
Eternity had already started.

But still,
It was with my arrival
That the jasmine behind the wall
Welcomed the memory of summer into its heart.
It was with my arrival

That, at six months old,
The garden's flowers
Turned to face winter
And yielded to the sound of tall black boots.

So, by the evidence of my trace,
Though my heart trembles with an unknown fear,
Though each year I grow older and quieter—
Deep within,
In the silent corner of my heart,
Where the rain's whisper
Does not steal sleep
From the garden's birds,

I wait, with an open heart,
For rain to fall upon the rooftop,
For the migratory birds in the alley
To delay their journey.

I want to stay,
With open hands,
To bring light into the home,
Far more than the hours I've let slip away.
I want to stay,
To see a sky heavy with rain,
And with an oceanic heart,
Bring the sea to life.

For the fish—our fish—
Belong to this body of ours.

June 2017

A Thousand Years of Sleep

For a thousand years, I slept,
In dreams of wings,
In dreams of dawn…
Like a butterfly, I fluttered,
Then flew away.
In that moment, I knew,
A thousand years passed,
Waiting, still,
With the hope of reunion.

Now, I stand here,
Wondering how to awaken
From my thousand-year slumber.
I long to walk once more
In the fragrant forest,
In the desert where the winds roam free,
To step into life,
And never count my steps again,
Carefree, forevermore!

Ah, the days in the distant village,
Where my heart was light and carefree!
How small and innocent was the world,
How easy the flowers bloomed in my hands,
How the sky of my heart soared high!

But today, my wings are buried
Under mountains of distant memories,
Resting in the quiet of time's embrace.

The Taste of Skepticism

The taste of skepticism,
I surrender to the early doubts,
To the laughter of the questioning sun,
As it passes through the half-closed eyes of doubt,
Until truth is proven or shattered,
And I surrender again.

Early mornings,
The air is uncertain, the chill of dawn sharp,
The taste of skepticism is… existence!
I push away the comfort of certainty,
To walk through the corridors of doubt,
From the silence of night to the chaos of day.

But still, in the crystal-clear light of reason,
I find myself lost,
For its clarity has already blended with my doubt!
Through the habit of staring at the sky,
That neither brightens nor darkens,
In that very moment,
When every being's movement begins,
What does its uproar mean in my heart?

Does sorrow, like the gaze of an uncertain soul,
Evaporate into a place where nothing else remains—

Where only the flight of uncertainty lingers?
It's curious,
On my birthday, I find myself unsure!
Knee to knee, I sit alone,
Revealing the secrets of my heart,
For on those days, even God knows
That doubt is the only story of our lives,
A story with no answers,
Where, from the first light of dawn to dusk,
I never close my eyes,
For it is all in His mystery!

Sometimes, with all my heart,
I offer my doubts into His hands,
Asking Him,
For the patience to endure,
And a little relief from the pain of waiting...

The Persimmon Tree

I remember how much I loved the scent of youth,
Like the fragrance of a jasmine flower mixed with the scent of persimmon trees,
Filling the yard of our house,
Where I would follow the breeze with longing,
Trying to preserve that breath of life for as long as I could.
But what a pleasant feeling it was!
My youth would pass, unaware of the cracked moments,
Years went by...
The persimmon trees, the bushes, and the sweet-smelling flowers remained,
My companions, through every season,
From the hot summer afternoons to the refreshing evening breezes.
The rush of water, the heated body of August's sun,
Bringing life and joy to the weary heart.
It was all so refreshing, so invigorating,
Walking through the earthy paths, my heart full of life,
And my soul consumed with the passion of youth!

I gathered countless memories from those days,
A basket full of fragrant dreams...
How wonderful those days were,
When every part of me longed for life and existence,
Time passed, and finally, those fragrant flowers bloomed again,
Now with no thorns or interruptions!
But the feeling I had when I realized

That the youth had left...
It had been a while since the sparrows had made their nests
By my window,
And every evening, before the sky darkened,
They would stick close to each other,
Their wings glittering in the last rays of sunlight,
Flying together, and then they'd disappear.
I've grown used to their sound,
Their hearts beating in time,
And from the cracks of their beaks,
They send messages to each other,
Their sparkling eyes speaking volumes.

Each night, before sleep,
Their presence behind my window
Has become a cherished habit,
And from there, I feel their peace, with all my being.
They know the responsibility of being sparrows well,
They fly through life, in sync with the rhythm of the world,
And even in the night, they don't forget their longing for peace and tranquility.
Like sparrows, we loved ourselves,
And never missed an opportunity to express our gratitude to life.
We shouted happiness from our hearts.
The sparrows understand that life is too short
To wait for the love we deserve,
To leave kindness and warmth for later.

I don't know if you ever felt this too,
As the warmth of time has hit us like waves,
But youth has long since passed,

And all that remains are memories.
I remember when I was a child,
And summer was only about death and travel,
And escaping from the long days,
Of hot summer and the endlessness of time.
Summer days were not just long; they were treasures of the soul.
From autumn to spring, each moment was rich with wonder,
I would look at the sky for hours, watching the birds fly,
Hoping to feel their joy,
As they passed by our home,
I prayed for the winds to carry my homemade kites,
Into the sky, lifting me up.

But the summer winds never came!
Now, summer is empty.
Its winds no longer carry joy,
Its warmth no longer nourishes the soul.
The days feel hollow,
And what remains of summer is only a memory,
Of fleeting moments and unanswered wishes.
Now, summer is only a story
Of what once was,
Of love lost in the waves of time,
And the stars in the sky seem far away,
As though they've forgotten us.
Now, in the silence of summer,
The heart doesn't play its song anymore,
For the warmth of the morning is forgotten,
And the summer wind no longer wakes the soul.

Fifty-Two and Still in My Homeland

I turned fifty-two and am still in my own homeland.
At two years old; five.
When I look into the depths of my life's hole,
My gaze becomes fixed on the wall of childhood...!
On the green leaves of boxwood...
On the kindness and childish friendships...
On the rush to grow up...
My gaze remains fixed;
On the carpet flowers...
In this deep hole, as I move forward,
My gaze becomes fixed on a sorrowful image...
The angry face of youth...
The face of the demon of destruction...
The face of jinn and darkness...
I remain transfixed
On a notebook,
On a poem full of pain...
My gaze wails
On the tall walls of the house
On the green leaves of the vines
Until my imagination,
In the depths of my mirage sky,
Can bring light to the warm stove of my home...
So that a word can settle in my heart:
"Staying"
And creating a garden full of events...
Living full of dew and chandeliers,
And weaving love,
In the fabric of "justice"...
At two years old; five.
Still – in this year worse than the pandemic year – I am seeking

To get through the isolation as quickly as possible!
I don't know what this yearning is to grasp the moments
and minutes of life in middle age!
On the other hand, I don't know what this stubbornness is,
To deepen the burning of these moments of middle age
and the oil lamp of my life!
If I had always dragged my bones on the rocky stones of
memories,
And the bitterness of life revealed its ugly face boldly,
This year,
The drum of sorrow beats across every village on this earth,
With the pretext of a raging wind, bringing plague and
misfortune,
Spreading its hidden, invisible shadow of destruction
And offering isolation to the villagers...
All angry and death-thoughtful, all on the edge of curses,
Shouting to the history of humanity:
"History, remember us..."
The precise space of my sorrowful imagination,
Is like a sparrow, trembling,
Fleeing from the fear of a black snake,
And the flickering flame of my thoughts, stuttering!
The dimension of the good memories of my life today
Belongs to the distant years,
When some of the young people of my village consider it a
mirage, a mere fantasy...!
The memory of contemporary history,
Has lost its short-term memory,
And has built a house of forgetfulness
Spanning all the villages of the world...!
Our minds are filled with doubt,
And the certainty of all is only found
In patience!
For thousands of years, we've been told:
The saviors pass through the path of patience...!

In this pretentious and hypocritical era of ours,
The face of nature, after all this neglect by humans,
Boasts and mockingly informs its chosen creatures,
That it is eternal.
Egoism and cruelty,
Spreading lies, anger, and hatred,
Have made it so that we are no longer concerned with birds,
Nor do we care about branches...!
The foundation of our life is crooked,
And yet we still think of the design of the wall...!
The lines of the wall of destiny,
Are full of withered dreams,
And the critics call the people of this era,
The burned and exhausted generation in this game of life...
In this galactic era,
Before we can bask in the breeze of our feelings,
A storm and thunder collapse upon us...!
And the simurgh of our thoughts,
With its wings unfurled, is struck down by the invisible arrow of human error,
Tired and worn,
In the division of words,
At the table of my imagination,
With a lantern in hand,
I continue to search for the cleansing and dusting of words like;
Truth, kindness, friendship,
And loving one another...
To shake the dust of years gone by,
From the mirror of the heart,
And in middle age, I will create a poem,
A fragrant one for humanity...!

June 2020

The Tale of Fifty-Three

Speaking of it is no easy task—
Behind the window of my gaze,
I hang my three-year-old self on a nail,
And kiss the four corners of the passing year,
Yet one truth cannot be denied:
"The weight of suffering has silenced me."

I've grown fearful…
Of wickedness and shallow stares
That creep to my very doorstep.
I retreat to the corner of my lonely room,
Adorned with longing and regret.
From shards of broken nights of waiting,
My feet are wounded, my hands ache.

I recall the courage I once had,
Sweeping away every cruelty as if dust.
And now, my wounded self—
How tenderly I once soothed it in the fountain of hope.
Make no mistake—
Today, at the close of three more years,
I've changed my fountain of hope!
Now, I hope for what lies ahead,
For the legacy I leave behind.

Slowly, I grow accustomed to ruin—
Yet in this ruin, I find freedom.
These days, even the birds of hope
Have flown away from the headlines of the papers.
Whether I will it or not,
Oblivion has come to find me.

Doctors say:
When oblivion takes hold,
First, it claims names, facts, and stories,
Then images,
And later, even feelings and emotions.

Even those consumed by forgetfulness
Forget their beloveds,
But never the scent of their clothing.
The sound of a cherished song,
Or a mother's lullaby,
Still draws a smile to their lips.
Faces and names fade into the fog,
But scents, touches,
And whispers of warmth—these remain.

They know the caress,
The kiss—but not the caresser, nor the kisser.

My ruin is the forgetting of names,
The forgetting of stories…
The stories I penned for the final chapters of my life.
But my freedom lies in this:
I have not forgotten my purpose,
The mission for which I still breathe.

I still remember the opening line

Of a beloved series from the '70s:
"Life is a prism in circular motion."
Back then, perhaps, we overlooked
The Eastern wisdom hidden within:
The cyclic geometry of time in its yearning,
The turning wheel, the dance of seasons.

But now, our modern minds
Embrace the Western tale of time—
Hegelian, linear, unbending.
And so, our notions of happiness,
Success, and progress follow suit—
A single line carved between birth and death.

Yet let us trace the circle and line
In the gentle wisdom of Anton Chekhov:
"The clock lies! Time doesn't turn in circles.
The idea of a circular clock is the work of a cunning sorcerer.
The true clock is an hourglass."
Grain by grain, it shows us what has fallen—
Never to return, like water that's flowed downstream.

Still, within the bowl of my eyes,
After all these years,
I see three photographs by a Danish artist—
Runners crossing the marathon's finish line.
They capture life as a race for progress and triumph,
A circle where one must run,
Outpace, break records, surpass.

And though, in these images,
There is a shadow of calm release—
Not satisfaction, but mere respite—

I see the faces, burning and worn from the contest.
Faces no different from those who see life
As a battlefield, a race to win.

Now, standing at the threshold of another year's end,
I must see life not as a race,
But as a prism in circular motion,
A dance of seasons.
I must rise above the clock and the calendar,
Above competition and contest—
For in the arena of time,
No one truly wins.

June 2021

Fifty-Four

In the year that passed,
As I slipped into my fourth decade,
Even on cloudy days,
I gazed at the sky with longing.
I spoke to no one of death, void, earthquakes, poverty, failure, or illness.
My only purpose in "life"—
The life that walked alone in the rain, under its umbrella—
Was to say, "We are happy."

Yet that very life didn't even ask my name,
And my happiness got lost in the winding alleys of the past year.
So I decided to ignore these numbers
That flow beside the house of my years,
To start anew each year.

Starting anew means selling the old samovar
And buying an electric kettle.
It means pinning a travel ticket
To the deed of my name and visiting again
Those who gave me the hope to stay alive.
It means staying silent about my weak heart
And wandering through sleepless nights,
Reaching a dawn filled with mint and mountain herbs.

I remember—
In youth, we exchanged endless questions with one another,
Humbly and patiently searching for a cool stream
To soothe our weary and exposed minds.
We awaited a miracle, hoping perhaps the door
Across the street might open,
And an angel would bring us a jar of wisdom,
A basket of insight.

Years came and went,
And we survived on this hollow hope.
Sometimes, we whispered to each other
Our seasonal despair:
What is this life?
Why do we paint its image on the white walls of alleys
Each morning,
Expecting our children not to scribble over it?

In the year that passed,
Sometimes I'd spend an entire day thinking of just one word—
I'd cast the word into the kiln of my mind.
The word would burn in the fire of my thoughts,
And I loved the scent of its ashes.
The fragrance of that word—
"Belonging"—
Was unlike any scent sold in the market.
But how can one explain a fragrance?
Especially the scent of "belonging"?

In the year that passed,
The elevators of "hope for life" in those around me had broken down.

From distant places, a song in the mode of Homayoun
Kept troubling our hearts,
And those who were meant to testify to our happiness
Had forgotten even how to smile,
Stuck at red lights in Tehran's crowded streets.

In the year that passed,
I lost the perfect time to feel joy
And to write in my beloved rough notebooks.
I waited through the cold for spring and summer,
Only for the broken branches of winter jasmine in spring
To turn my heart to autumn once again.
I embraced my loneliness and carried it home,
Careful along the way
That the secret of life would not slip from the beak of my fortune bird,
Fall to the street,
And be trampled by unsuspecting passersby.

And again,
In the year that passed,
Anxious and restless,
I wandered the winding alleys in search of "happiness."
Even as the full-length mirror in my home
Reflected a mocking image of regret back at me.

In the year that passed,
Though I built the world of my poetry
With bricks of truth and mortar of love,
I refuse to take a souvenir photo with it—
Because the behind-the-scenes images are gray,
And none of the crew is smiling.

How wonderful it is when fear sometimes steps aside,

Allowing the world to transform, if only briefly,
Into a basket of vivid strawberries,
Bouquets of narcissus,
And a road leading deep into the forest.
Such moments were rare in the past year,
But they were enough.
In those fleeting instants,
I was happy,
And my horizon of hope grew brighter.

In the year that passed,
Some nights were heavy with darkness,
Drenched in sorrow and rain.
The umbrella was broken,
But my shirt was pure white—
Just like thirty years ago,
When I fell in love with the tiles
Of Sheikh Lotfollah Mosque in Isfahan,
And read coffee fortunes with Armenian women of Jolfa,
Hoping to spark a fire
To extinguish doubt and despair.

Praise be to God—
My flashlight still has batteries.

June 2022

The Window

When I open the window,
I'm taken back to the village.
I was a child then—
We had gone to the countryside.
What a joy it was—
Its summers,
Its sunlight,
Its shade,
The soft caress of its air.

A stream,
Whispering,
Flowing past the trees.

On the second floor of a grand old house,
By a window that stretched from ceiling to floor,
We sat together.

The cool breeze of mountains and trees
Drifted in, filling the room.

When I close the window,
I find myself in the grandest hotel,
On the forty-eighth floor.
I see the finest objects,
A breakfast table adorned with everything imaginable.
I savor it all—
The presence, the essence—
Taking the greatest pleasure in what is.

The window,
It is still the same window…

Breathe Deeply

You ask,
In other times and places,
Is it possible to belong?

Please,
Take a deep breath.
Think inwardly.
Fasten knowledge, experience, and memory
Together with care.

Look into the mirror,
Face to face with yourself,
Bound by duty,
Obliged by honesty,
Speak—
Say it aloud,

In a voice so steady,
That when
Your eyes meet mine,
I am utterly disarmed,
Held captive by the salt of your truth.

From behind the curtain of reality,
Honestly,
The careless chatter of our tongues
In describing unfamiliar horizons
Holds far more delight.

Behind the Beautiful Mask of Exile

Behind the beautiful mask of exile,
Behind its seemingly acceptable reversal,
The philosophy of life
Struggles in the mind...
And I,
In a fierce battle,
Like a fire igniting in a haystack—
The result of a lifetime of effort—
How empty my hands are...!
My soul wounded by the blade of ignorance...
For hypocrisy and deceit
Have become the sustenance of the people of my time.
The vileness of mankind
Has plundered the minds of the children of my homeland,
While exile, separation, and alienation
Are favored over staying, loving, and embracing...
I do not know... my hands are empty
To build an anchor,
To spread a dreamlike bed,
To create and sing again a love song
To reach the dawn of reunion...

Raining

Rain is falling,
And I linger behind the glass,
Veiled by lace,
Breathing deeply the storm within—
Whirlpools stirring in my soul,
Waves of tempest,
Secrets swept by southern winds,
The humid sigh of a sultry dawn.

Hours drift soft as silk,
A fury smolders, fierce yet futile,
And still…
A love, long buried,
An ache without end,
Carved into the fading pages
Of my dust-bound calendar.

Searching for a wall

I'm searching for a wall
where a wild rose might grow,
one visible enough
to offer a reason to lean
into the memory of this summer.
Don't blame me,
for the flowers of my gardened heart
were given to others,
and my gaze turned…
toward winter.

Oh, how I wish
I didn't know how much you are,
or how deeply understanding your being is meant.
But between us, there lies such distance,
that even the breeze from our street
never reaches yours.
Even the migratory birds of our lane
have delayed their journey,
waiting beneath your wings
to change the seasons.

Ah… they too, are thinking of a place
that doesn't exist!
Like the stars in the sky,
searching for something,
growing older and quieter with each passing year.

Don't mistake it…
I too,
when it comes to the forgotten times,
no longer feel my hands reaching or my heart longing.
The lines upon my forehead
stand as proof of this claim.
These days,
waiting without color
always brings pain…

My Tangled Threads

The threads of my affairs are tangled!
And I,
with strands of my flawed past,
tainted by loneliness and deprivation,
am forced
to delay the entirety of my life…
At the threshold of autumn,
with hair turned white,
amidst the grass, the ponds, and the imagined pheasants of our past,
I still carry the spring in my mind,
with a slender hope
to reach the impossible dreams we once held…

I stand in the street,
watching time pass me by.
I cling to this moment,
so time might flow past me easily
(and not carry me away…)
And after time has passed,
I will fulfill my vow in the street!

To which bird shall I offer a grain of my vow?
All the birds were in need of seeds…
I wish to lie to you!
Lies like these:

That at night,
the sound of seagulls keeps me awake!
Which seagulls?
Which sea?
I live in this building with a 60-meter yard,
where the sky
can barely be seen in its blue.
A building where even its windows face the street,
full of the presence of cars...

Oh, how I wish
someone could bring me the image of seagulls—
one tapping the window with its beak,
another nesting on a branch of a tree—
where I could offer them grains,
and they would not leave until fed.
And that other bird,
who brings straw from dawn to dusk
so we might have a nest...

Yes,
all those birds,
I would bring them into my poem…
And two or three gardens full of flowers—
but still,
the threads of my affairs are tangled…

My Solitude

Someone once told me:
"Everything about you has become mathematics...!
Everything about you has become geometry...!"
And sighed,
Unable to solve the equation.
I said to him:
"My relationship with others
Has three sides!
The first side: me
The second side: others
The third side:
is my solitude!
The more I lose hope in others,
The more I take refuge in that third side..."

I Wish

I wish someone
Forever,
Would build a bridge between my heart and my eyes
So that I
Could take shelter behind my love
And shift the boundaries of the world
For them!

My Homeland

I have a homeland
In the most storm-prone spot on earth...
Do you know where I speak of?
You wouldn't believe it...
A place where, as much as I love it,
It doesn't love me back...!
A place where
Every day
Trust breaks...
Hope fades...
And always
It gets too late!
I don't leave,
But it has no claim on me,
Though I belong to it...
I know the ways through the ruins
And
The shared glances of being together...
But,
It does not open its arms...!

The Fields of Sleep

Autumn hasn't arrived,
Yet beneath my feet,
I see the autumn leaves!
I hear the sound of leaves,
Yellowed and falling from the trees…
On the paths we walk, there is always a multitude of leaves!
And a multitude of people,
Who, under the rain that hasn't come yet,
Cannot hide the leaves…
But their pains,
They hide well!
For in my land,
The fields of "sleep" are vast,
Autumn hasn't come,
And everyone seeks to possess geranium pots…
But I,
I don't know how to cover all this pain and deprivation,
With geranium flowers and a single hyacinth pot on the balcony?
But I do know,
One day,
Ultimately, these pains and anxieties will rise,
And free themselves from behind the geraniums and hyacinths,
Their freedom will unveil the sorrow of all…
Then,
The ones who pass by each other,
Will no longer distance themselves from each other's sorrows…

The Sea

I descended towards the sea
On the gentle slope,
In the warm, humid air of Fujairah, it felt strange.
After twenty minutes of walking, face to face with the sea,
Suddenly, I saw it!
I passed the alleys of yesterday,
And my soul was lost to today!
I remembered six years ago, Mohamed Plassi, with his usual kindness,
Gifted me three words: "the shore" and "the sea."
Tonight, I uttered his words again, and then saw the sea and its shore.
I remembered Mohamed's flight, soaring to the sky.
I didn't have colored pencils to sketch the sea, all twisted and bent!
I wished I were a good artist, to paint the face of Ernest Hemingway – who had come to Fujairah,
With an angel by his side, towel in hand, constantly wiping his forehead,
He was by the shore, looking at an old man lost to the sea.
I looked at the sky...
Its blue, like the blue of the sea, was dark and night-like.
I told Mohamed:
I saw Hemingway and an angel by the shore!
He replied: For thirty-one years, I've grown old in the sea,
So many fish caught with them!

Night fell…
I turned my back to the sea, burning with heat.
It had been years since I had forgotten the words "sea" and "shore,"
And the fear of drowning in the night had faded from my mind.
The smell of fish and the sound of waves
Had stirred up echoes behind my walk,
And I lifted my steps higher…
In the hotel restaurant, the waiter brought me cold fish,
I didn't understand how he knew I wouldn't eat that night!
I held my sleep tightly in the cold hotel room,
And I wanted to know deeply,
Could I, too, survive four days and nights, like the old Cuban fisherman of Hemingway,
And fish for a giant marlin with my hook?

August 2022
Fujairah, UAE

The Flower of Doubt

Passing is impossible...
Through the towering walls of distrust!
To leap over this ever-growing wall,
Our thoughts,
Have no wings to fly...
These days,
The longing to soar
Is a great absence among us!
The body and soul of the city
Is empty of human resolve...
All are behind the wall,
Wounded,
Imprisoned in their own waiting...
Only a hidden belief,
Is a light at the bottom of our being,
To make the impossible possible,
And to open the fountain of trust
Up to the heavens,
And to dry the flower of doubt
In the garden of hope...
And then,
I will shout; believe me... believe me... believe me...

The Color of Truth

The colorful promises of people,
Drawn from dreams they can never reach,
Are endless...!
The tales and endless epics,
In their beliefs,
Have taken on the color of truth...!
I,
Remain silent...
I step back...
Mesmerized by the eagerness in their eyes,
Born of their ignorance,
I stare…!
I look at their years without spring,
The footprints they leave
In a winter without snow...
At the paths they take
Through the sorrowful nights
Of their followers…
When you leaf through their life's book,
Page by page,
It will be all white…
Without effect...
In the spring of sleep,
I lie toward the breeze…
I have fallen asleep!
For the joy of the rain that falls,

And bestows on me the change of seasons…
Alas,
I was in the pursuit of a tomorrow,
Which became the regret of my today,
And all my longings,
Inconsiderately,
I placed upon its shoulders…
The melody of rain,
Softly,
From the window of my spring sleep,
Settles on me like velvet,
And the fragrance of orange tree embraces,
Spreads my salvation
On the bed of the night…
In this midnight,
At the start of autumn,
My spring-sleep room
Became a room of poetry, a sight to behold…
The flowers of my poems,
Like the beloved of the night,
Bloomed from the freshness of the rain's honesty…
I say plainly,
In the language of my land's thirst,
My breaths come alive…!
And from the events unfolding before my eyes,
My throat tears open from silence…!
I am not dead yet,
But it seems,
All the senses of my body,
In collusion with the spirit beneath my skin –
Like steam on a mirror,
Have mocked the very legitimacy of my existence…
It seems I have been lost…!
The night, from the crowd of voiceless sounds,
Does not awaken any feeling in me,

And the days,
I wait
To scorch my shoulders in the sunlight
And revive my sense…!
But,
On my pulse,
I hear no steady beat,
And in the ebb and flow of turbulent words,
From the window facing the street,
I gaze at my homeland…
At the games that have begun from this point…
I wish the world would realize its mistake and
Take a deep breath,
And not set an end date for our lives…!

September 2022

The Bipolar Forms of My Being

The bipolar shapes of my existence,
In the sway and weave of my thoughts,
Creep insidiously,
And I,
Am left behind…!
The thickness of the ignorance of my era,
Has become a platform
For the excuses of migrating birds…
The recurring moments,
Between the inner and outer realms of my land,
Between Iran and the hallways of my home,
My prayers spill out
Through the window of weariness,
And only
Shards of crystal
Rest upon the palms of my hands…
I don't know if my separation
From the bond that is always bright in my mind,
Will ever fade away?

September 2022

Asking Me

They ask me,
With my silence,
To shout out my liberations...!
To give thanks
For welcoming poems
That still remain unsaid in my mind...!
So that in the dreams of others,
I may carve a space,
And create
The most elusive image
For their loneliest soul
In the frame of their eyes...!
Apparently, they do not know;
Though running is not within me,
My dreams, like birthday candles,
Do not extinguish with a single breath...!
I pay the price,
But only for my laziness.
I only
Give meaning to my mind,
To my soul,
Through my dreams,
And if
I do not reach them,
I become a body
That merely breathes...!
I,
With my silence,
Do not rejoice...!

Sensation

Our memory,
With a body worn by dust and thirst,
Does not recall a pure sensation!
In the confusion of the shadows of the night,
I searched for a flame of light
To lose the reflection of the shadows on the surface of the pond
Before the mirror...
The winds;
Carry the memories away,
So that humanity
Becomes the singularity of its own songs...!
It becomes neutral and
Offers the souls tainted by dust
To life...
May it be that
The scent of decay
From the passing clouds of our lives
Reaches the joyful noses...
I've shouted too much;
I want a pure feeling, a lasting one...
Even if,
In the hunt for the moon,
The truth of my imagination
Clutches my throat
And
Bites into my neck,
Shaking my shirt
In my skin...
With my charred hands,
I do not search for diamonds,
But;
I do not forget our reason...

A Thick Book

You don't know
How thick the book of my knowledge has become,
A volume where not a single line can be read...!
Half a century
Has passed since the grazing of the pages I've read,
And still,
The thought of diving into the water
Is nowhere to be found in my mind!
In fact, I fear
The water may pass over me,
And I would surrender my lost tranquility
To the chaos that follows...!
Indeed,
In my certainty,
"Hope" has not planted a seed in the "field of improvement"...
I reprimand myself,
Don't worry...
But distant and near memories
Shout at me,
Year by year... not even last year...!

December 2022

Butterflies

The Omen of Rainfall
The window
Freed itself from the company of the ugly and vile flies...!
Rain
Made the window its companion,
To remind it
Of the wandering of butterflies,
The tune of the wandering musician,
And those
Drunken memories
That became legends...!
The window is silent,
The window is closed,
The window is fearful,
Fearful of the dread of winter,
Winter of waiting...
Even the kiss of rain
Does not take its gaze
Beyond the quiet, empty alleys,
Beyond the gaze fixed on the silent doorframe.
The devotion of the window
In waiting
Has no end,
And the anxiety of not arriving
Sits always
Within its frame...!
The window longs for
The wait...

Unseen Dreams, Unlived Hopes

Dreams never had,
Nights never seen,
Desires never reached the mind,
Have become
The curse upon us humans...!
A truth

that never existed -
Has so hidden itself
Within our being,
That we ourselves
Cannot find it...!
Unaware
Of all the memories
We have never had...!
The ones that have become
The lump in our throats!
Attachments that we were never meant to hold,
Sanctified,
And the guilt
Has taken root in every cell of our being...!
A great toll,
This deep hole
In our destiny...!

March 2022

The Sweetness of Losing Time

How delightful it is
To lose time
In the heart of life...
Forgetting the passage of days
In travels and cafés...
Forgetting all the opportunities
In the exuberance of youth...
And now...
In the autumn season of life,
Time seeks its revenge on me...!
Wherever I step in this city,
I find myself suffering,
In inadequacy and discomfort,
In my condition...
Without reason or explanation,
In the turmoil of the world,
The chains of distant desires and dreams
Have been made forbidden in me...!
My inner strength
Has led me
To a humility beyond words,
Guiding me to a path
Of pursuit and striving...!
I,
Am content
With this breaking of the heart...!

My Sealed Words

The cage of my sealed words
Is a monument to my swallowed rage...
Unbloomed words, stifled by the insincerity of mankind,
In an era of fire, discord, and blood,
In a time
Where love and kindness
Have parted ways,
No tune for love or romance
Rises from me...
No whisper but silence
Settles behind the window of my throat.

I remain unheard—
Until the dust-covered window of my solitude,
Until this chest, compressed with pain,
Opens itself to the sun,
Shattering the chains of doubt,
And joyfully
Roars with liberation...
Only then,
Can I recount the story of this prison
To those
Who, beneath their skin,
Are still standing tall.

My Dreams Were Born

When my dreams were born,
When I gave my mind
Wings to soar—
To break free from the cocoon of loneliness—
I sought "liberation"...
But
Labyrinths of dead-end paths
Deepened the chasms of my unreachable dreams,
And the prophets of my mind
Stood face-to-face with a coffin
That bore the weight of "failure."

Trust is absent...
I know,
In the stormiest place on earth,
My flight will find no companion in reaching.
This, I have come to understand...

Being Alive Because of the Dream

Sometimes I live in dreams!
Sometimes, in that ancient awakening!
Sometimes I am alive for wandering in the solitude of myself,
And sometimes I live in my absence from so many places...

Through the weary eyelids of my worldview,
With a stutter in my gaze and speech,
I've kept hope
Behind the dull, faded curtain of my naïve optimism,
Hoping the belief in rain
Will soften
The interplay of moonlight and bars.

If I didn't share in your tears,
If I only
Became the toll of your outcry,
My reason was
The overdrawn tally of my awakenings.

Yet still,
I am alive because I believe in the rain.

Natural and ordinary

Perhaps we must believe
That all these happenings,
All these losses,
All these dreadful events,
Are but a simple occurrence...!
Natural and ordinary
In this endless world...!

Perhaps we must,
With frozen faces,
Look at the tears and wails
As if they were
Tea dregs,
And think only of the sweetness of sugar...!

Perhaps the world's compulsion
Cannot be overturned...!
If that is so,
Then no one
Should speak to me again of light, rain, or serenity,
Of purity, kindness, or prayer...
No one
Shall entangle me with expectations, love, embraces, or affection!

Certainties all turn to doubt,
And when we meet beneath the sky,

It is our image, our shadow,
That walks the streets...

What words become strangers...
Any place could be mine,
Yet now is not!
Homeland
Becomes the most foreign word in our minds...
And we no longer smile,
Even at our shared pasts...!

My Heart

How childlike,
My heart is seduced…!
By the circuits of my brain,
That constantly
Spark within my head…!

When, in the sculpted endurance of night,
No pillow
Murmurs the cries of love,
When
No dregs of coffee
Awaken a voice of consciousness,
When
No clock—even the hourglass—
Fulfills the promise of waiting…

The green thirst of my heart
Is drained…
Its legs become frail,
Panting rapidly,
Yearning to savor its childlike pool
Before it reaches the dripping faucet of life…

It knows better than anyone
How to stay true to its shape.

November 2022

On the Other Side of the Wind

Across the wind,
The trembling throat of my imagination
No longer releases its voice
To the ears of the sky...!

For as much as I deepened,
The patience of ears
Overflowed, unwilling to bear
The echo of my song...

The gaze of eyes
Chased my glance
Along the trails of unseen crossings...

The mirror of the swamp's surface
Is deceitful, drawing eager eyes toward it.
And I—
I do not know, I do not know
In which water
To wash away my lingering anxieties.

My name,
Untouched by freshness,
Has grown stale.
My memory,
Poisoned.

And the miracle of life-giving melodies,
I no longer
Hear them from my lips.

Colorful Promise

The colorful promises of people
That take their hue from unreachable dreams,
Have no end…!

The endless tales and epics,
In their beliefs,
Truth wears its colors…!

I remain silent…
I have promised,
To remind them of their past promises,
I stand at a distance…
Gazing into their eyes,
Born of their ignorance,
I stare…!

I look at their years without spring,
The footprints they left
In a snowless winter…
The path they walked
Through the sorrowful nights of their followers…

You know…
When you flip through the pages of their life,
Page by page,
It will be white—white,
Without any impact.

Blessed is the Remedy Forever

Blessed is the cure that lasts forever...
Blessed is the sweetness of emerging from all hardships...
The union with the promised home and the companion of the journey...
Blessed is the rise of the most beautiful moon in dreams...
The absolute silence of watching
And the fragrant breath of light...
Blessed is
The clear certainty and freedom from doubts...
Relief from futile longing and the softening of truths...
Blessed is
The final outcome of fate and the chance of reunions...
The last line of imagination and the blossoming of wishes...
Blessed is
Reaching the alley of love and engraving love in the mind...
Becoming dew in a gaze
And knotting in sobs...
Blessed is
Passing through everything forbidden and all fears...
Surviving the storm and lightening the moments...
How simple... how distant... how near...
This has always been the way of time...
Blessed, blessed, is the relief from all this worry and fatigue...

My Voice

I have reached a point
Where my voice has turned to resin...
Cold and stony...
A stone that
With every year added to my life
Becomes harder and harder...
My voice has become a thread these years,
It spreads over
Pieces of my being, like ice,
I have reached a point
Where in my contracted sanctuary,
I perceive invisible presences...
From within...
Alive in the tomb of breath,
I moan in my frozen skin...
I have reached a point
Where, on the walls of alleyways,
With an unreadable script,
I write every day:
Do not hurry...!

My Mind's Frame

Blood, like molten lead in the stream of my veins,
My tired veins ran...
I was weary,
So much so that the fatigue of my ancestors
Had hammered migration into patience
In the wheat fields.
But today,
My patience,
Like a soul long passed,
Strikes the whip of my veins!
And the crumbling walls of my city
Depict the faces of my ancestors
In the frame of my mind...
The distance,
Like a filthy scourge,
Flows through the alleys of generations!
The alley lonelier than the myth of solitude,
Its cold breath is carried by the wind...
The echo of the steps of generations
Is with me on the ancient roads of my city,
And in the howling wind,
The trees and birds
Whisper songs of sorrow and mourning...
I, weary and tired,
Call out to the lost parts of myself
On the empty paths of the night,
It was wind and wind...
Again, steadfast and elephantine,
I called the fossils of the night,
Motionless in the line of the wind...
It was night and doubt,
Doubt had been polished
In the alley of my mind...

Steps

At the end of all this impossibility,
All these maybes and doubts,
Whether walking the path,
Or staying in the refuge,
It doesn't matter...
I see no difference...
A mind that howled for me
For half a century,
Its legs
Do not take a step forward...
If I had any luck,
It has led me here.

April 2022

Spring

The wind, the sound of geranium pots,
The smell of food from the oil lamp,
The familiar tone of a harmonica,
All emerged from the layers of my old memories,
From the folds at the corner of my eyes,
From all the veins of my being,
On a spring Friday afternoon,
It settled within me...
Calmly,
I walk through the streets of my youth – which no longer exist –
To be freed from despair and deprivation...
I pass through gates adorned with flowers
To find myself in the spring rain,
On the stones and bricks I have laid over thirty years,
On the porches and towers I have built,
To plant wild rose vines,
And sometimes in the week,
I hang the laughter of children and the candies of hope on the white walls of the alley...
I live in spring,
Drenched in its colors,
Even with dreams that
Have not yet sprouted from the earth,
I live to the fullest...!
I am reborn in spring...

March 2023

Outcome

I killed my mouth...!
For its words,
For its outcome,
Did not become a bridge to shorten the distance...!
From that moment,
I feel
Something within me has sprouted,
Something like tears...!
Something like the growing of a blade of grass
In the warm belly of existence...
I know this killing has its own retribution!
Its punishment,
A tender growth full of mystery, with a thousand passions,
Is in my heart...
It grows,
It grows from above...
I feel like I'm sitting on a mound
And with open fists,
I claim the earth with pride
As my own...!
I feel that love,
Like a river of light,
Like the wave of longing,
Makes the darkness of my life deteriorate...!
I killed my mouth
To feel that love
Is born with my coming into being...!

Debate

This September wants
To throw me into the clamor of autumn...
It is September, and the winds signal the change of season...
But I,
Still caught up in the twisting and turning of
Summer's dark nights...!
The relentless, fierce winds of autumn
Have not yet arrived,
And the green embrace of the trees,
In an enticing dusk,
Denies me...
This year, I want
To entrust the old anxieties of my autumn
To the allure and intoxication of the crunching walk
On the colorful streets of Tehran,
Without the concerns of the future or the many ailments,
And end each morning with fragrant miracles,
Debating love and nothingness.

First day *(In memory of the late Mortaza Mehrain, who created memories for me for over thirty years...)*

First day
I said to myself: he's gone...
I will never see him again.
On the second day, I repeated it,
But with hesitation and doubt,
The same old, recurring story of shipwrecked souls...
The third day passed as well,
And amidst the sound of shadowy winds,
This certainty came to me,
With a heavy voice:
Your distant dream is becoming closer,
My scent waves there,
It's there... amidst the white flowers of remembrance...
I,
Am in my river... though I left that land...
In the flames of my being,
Don't you remember the mad, restless soul within me?
Don't you recall the caged, protesting bird, knocking on the walls?
Poor thing, searching for a crack,
Walking through my being, tiring itself out...
I listened to its voice,
Heard the liquid pain of its cry,
I heard its weeping late at night...
Transformed... ashamed,
My heart trembled in my chest,
Like the heart of a fawn,
I called it,
With the intoxicating fragrance of night-blooms,
My voice, that trembling voice...
Amidst the weeping, so much, so wailing...
I told it, I love you, don't you recognize me?

My eyes smell of sorrow, can't you see me?
Its voice... but not trembling,
Not out of doubt, ambiguity, or implication,
Its sound,
Though it came from a distant world,
Yet it was within me... within the very fiber of my being...
Like a vine, its echo reached,
Why, then, do you weep so senselessly for me?
What do you know of this circle I bear?
My circle of fate,
Here, as it became fortunate, it became my life's circle,
In a moment,
I split the boundaries of worlds,
Sadly, I packed my belongings from that world,
Until I reached the spring of distant gardens,
My vessel of thought, found calm,
In the night of luminous meetings...
I don't know where I am,
But I know,
I'm far from the ungrounded joys... far...
I sit here waiting,
Perhaps one day you will come to visit me...
But until then,
Say with your love,
Like loyal lovers, tell me,
Of that eternal lover's realm,
Those fruits of light, that crystal palanquin...
May it be delightful for you... may it be delightful for you,
The drunkenness of your passionate longing,
Your song of madness,
May it be blessed for you... may it be blessed for you,
The day of your birth, joyful,
In the sky of your new existence...

June 2022

I Keep Thinking

I keep thinking
I've left something behind
on the other side of my dreams...
Yet the flames of thought's echo
shake the silence of my darkened home,
and the sharp edges of my nights,
etched deep in the soil of my town,
grind my breath to dust.

Moment by moment,
only mess and confusion remain
in the haze of my dreams...
In these dreams,
I wander streets filled with illusions,
streets—seemingly intoxicated by their roots...
Rain-soaked and cold,
these streets lay bare,
heavy with a pain I can't escape.

In the spaces between sleep,
I hear my voice from afar,
a sound both familiar and fractured—
chewed, not chewed,
calling to itself,
yearning for a spark of light.
I see the pens in my mind's stalls,
where terrified memories graze,

chewing thoughtlessly,
haunted by echoes long past.

The logic of my dreams,
mute and buried,
drips through my waking hours,
lost in sentences with verbs but no time.

Yet, in the midst of this noise,
my patience cries out,
whispering the truth:
Exile, my friend,
is never as far as it seems...

Purely Fate

The world is entirely fate,
and it doesn't even care about its own story...
It cannot be blamed
for not being there when they named me,
and my soul had no idea
how I stepped into the world,
and I didn't know
that my place
was never meant to be here...

I didn't know... I didn't understand,
that I should listen, spring by spring,
to the lies of the sparrows,
and never settle at a dead-end.
I didn't know
that in every stone, a spell exists,
and that water is only a memory,
and that a bird,
never ages in the reflection of its flight...

I didn't know
that I couldn't stay indifferent,
and constantly tell myself:
This is the road that passes,
and all you need to do,
is shake the dust off the steps of those who have gone

before you—
who are already destined to leave—
and steal your gaze
from the creases by your eyes,
the crooked smile of your lips,
and the tears of longing trapped inside,
and instead,
fix your eyes on a poet's notebook,
whose author lies awake through the night...

The world is purely fate...
Whatever the rain was,
we went beneath it.
Whatever the wind was,
we cried out within it.
Whatever the path was,
it led us astray.
Whatever lips there were,
we cursed the kiss upon them.
Whatever companions we had,
we lost our way with them,
until we finally saw
the destination, alone...
Until we held the sky
in our arms, alone,
and forever,
gazed into the clarity of the water,
alone...

Thunderstorms

The domains of lightning's rain
over the land of the tribe of refugees,
no longer left a brick standing,
nor a turquoise gem...!
The foolish repetition of history
has dried up the lakes...
Old vultures
peck at the souls of mankind...
From the pit of the reed flute,
the people's cries of God is no longer heard...
The silence of enlightened metaphors,
those of expired thinkers,
has left the longing to smell the moon's scent
as a memory in the hearts...
The simple-minded fools,
have become vengeful butterflies,
and they have cut the branches
of the citron tree to its roots...!

But in this very commotion,
I know in the end,
the tired night,
regretful of the massacre of the roofless pigeons,
will come...
and the blind owl,
uneasy and mad,
will go in search of usurped dreams...

I see the tranquility of the mirror,
which has been neutralized in the lightning,
perched on the branch of a tree,
the sieve of the sieve,
a canary sits...
For
this lantern of the village must be kept lit,
so the migratory birds
can find their way home...

Nirvana

Autumn and the cawing of crows
– who only know how to scratch the soul
with their voices
and place a saw
on the wounded throat...! –
reminds me
of ancient miniature paintings...!
Paintings with people of squinted eyes
and backgrounds of faded yellow and blue...
Cypress trees, compared to the height of humans,
have never really grown tall,
and in the rain that never came,
they try to appear vibrant...!

I don't mince words,
and openly say:
I despise both of them!
I don't know,
it seems as if an earthquake is about to happen,
or maybe it already has, and many have died,
which is why the world
has become so soulless...!
There's no one to tell these people,
on the deck of this world's balcony,
a man
smelled a petunia
and tossed his dreams into the air...

He
was the captain of a ship,
a great ship, to sail through the waves of the sea...
He bears the cradle of these vast seas on his shoulders...
But
when I stood beside him,
he didn't say anything from within,
he fell silent and... left!
It seems that at that moment
he became a dream in the prime of his youth...
He no longer speaks
for the rest of his life,
he settles in dreams
until after his silence,
he lends
the petunia of his dreams...
so that after his departure,
with the fragrance of love,
he may reach Nirvana
in every drop of autumn rain...

Everything Will Be Fine

Where, then, are your dreams?
What happened to all your beautiful rainbows
that you've buried in the soil?
Why have your days
become so strangely faithless,
your eyes fixed only on the path of bread,
and a date to sweeten your taste?

Perhaps
we shouldn't, in the terror of words,
seek something resembling a miracle
in the ashen faces of aged counselors,
those who endlessly advise us to endure,
and constantly say, "Everything will be fine."

Let it Linger

I struck a warning at the yellow dawn of the window:
Let patience come; let sleep linger...!

In the vestibule of my home,
I remembered:
The pain within me
is a door left open—
yet no one passes through it.

In the longing for movement, for release,
words fail to describe it—
how overflowing patience truly is...

Amid the repetition of hollow promises,
no birth smiles,
and in the lament of memories,
we are only left
to mourn, trembling,
the flight of laughing voices.

Swallow

I have become the traveler of shadow and light,
following the wings of a restless swallow—
one that passes through the blade of chance,
seeking a knot of sun
to land on a roof
with the language of thirst.

The harsh clarity of the wind,
the tender faith of rain—
I've carried them both
behind the weary eyelids of the world.

To greet a morning with a whispered hello,
or summon a memory
in the slow breadth of life—
I have written them, unadorned,
on the blackboard of the village school of my soul.

I have written countless lessons for others.
Unpaid,
I've even composed essays:
Subject: Free choice
Writing: Mandatory

Why can't the world be overturned?
Humanity was cast to earth
before words were ever born—
for if, from the moment their head touched the ground,
they cried out:
The world... the world... the world.

New Horizons

The hammer of the clock
strikes my life so cunningly.
How restless it slips a stick
into the wheels of my laughter.
And how jarringly it rubs its head against the door,
dragging the night
into the heart of my home.

I turn off the lights,
draw the curtains,
close the doors—
hoping another door
will open before me.

Before my world
is filled with dead-end streets,
before my mind,
heavy with memories,
recalls only wounds and scars,
before I
tighten the noose of life
around myself.

As long as there is still
a flicker in someone's gaze,
as long as the garden of dreams
still carries the scent of orange blossoms—
let us open a path,
and walk toward new horizons.

Keepsake Photography

On the very day I was born,
I wished to drive my fingers
into the malicious cracks of the world,
to stop its leaks
from soiling even the folds of my swaddle.

From that moment onward,
on every cursed day,
at the sight of a dry leaf upon the earth,
unbidden,
a sorrow settled into my heart.

In the bitter days of solitude,
at every sight of ingratitude,
unwillingly,
a regret weighed down my sighs.

On nights where I breathed in isolation,
on those same nights
when I heard the whispers of the dead
rising from their coffins,
on those nights
when the branches of grapevines
entwined themselves with graves,
the only anchor of my patience
was a keepsake photograph—
the memory of the day I was born.

Fiery Season

This autumn,
is a little "love" indebted to us.
I gave it a chance
to pay its debt and not leave us "without water"…
So that this "fiery" season
may strike its "love"
into the heart of November.
I honestly don't know
in what time or
on which land
"love" became the share of fall.

Breathing You In

To speak of you in impromptu verse,
I need a river
dancing through its bends...
A sun
untouched by any moon…
And at once,
a forest dense and full,
yet bearing no fruit.

Then,
I could speak of you
for the rest of my days—
becoming a sparrow
who has found its way to a granary of wheat.
I'd become
the poet of the city…

I'd write:
How does the wind know you?
How does the rain recognize you?
What wisdom does the light hold
to find your footsteps
and make them a sacred path?

I speak of you in improvisation,
write you line by line,
wander through the alleys of life,
pass through moonlit dreams and reveries,

to delight in the spoils of the moments
you have crafted for me.

When,
in the radiance of your being,
in the rhythm of your loving heart,
in the fragrance of your presence,
in the tenderness of your gaze,
in the melody of your beautiful voice—
I breathe,
and endlessly speak of you in impromptu verse.

Whispers

Eyes,
Hands—
no mere tale of familiarity...
Such richness they hold,
such boundless grace,
that wilted narcissus blooms,
severed from their stems,
can still,
by the fragrance of "remembrance,"
be revived within a living mind.

In this autumnal age,
may it never come to pass—
a world
where neither the narcissus is recalled
nor we ourselves...
For if it does,
our twilight shall march
toward oblivion.

My hands are empty,
yet love bears witness:
I could not bring
all the ocean
or all of hope
into our home.

My whispers filled the street:
Where is autumn?
Where... is it?
Where is the one
who called out to us
halfway along the road?
Where... is my spring?

Delicate Petals

I inhale the sweet fragrance of understanding
from your being,
for you have sown hundreds of colorful excuses
within others.
You,
like a flower blooming in the wasteland,
slowly unfurl your delicate petals,
stretching lazily,
and with joy, step into the newly awakened world of awareness
to claim it all as your own!
You place them in the vase of knowledge,
watering them with your love and wisdom,
in hopes that, one day, they will grow into sturdy trees,
and with your hands raised to the sky in prayer,
you seek what is needed!
This is how pain must be healed,
so that it no longer hurts.

Pomegranate's Crack

The world has taken on a stench
of hypocrisy and decay...
And I,
at the beginning of the new year,
in my fifties,
still feel the ache of believing
that the world can be calmed,
that liars can be exposed...
That it is possible
to not only think of the bread for hungry children,
but to speak to them of love,
and release them from the terror of the pomegranate's crack...
We can entrust them
to a sky filled with pomegranate stars...
The truth is
that in this world,
everyone has a lost dream of their own,
carrying the weight of waiting – forever, with pain –
on their shoulders,
and all of us
are bound to preserve this fruitless longing...!

Sorrow On Sale

In the years that passed,
The shops of our city
Had put sorrow and grief on sale,
Plenty of it, at a cheap price...!
It was inexpensive, with an expiration date set for the day,
And its time of consumption was limitless...!
Both the wholesalers and the retailers
Filled your basket according to your ability and purchasing power...!
What amazed me was that
The people of our city
Never went anywhere else,
And in these stores,
Day and night,
They hoarded sorrow and grief...
As if there was nothing else in the world to buy,
Except the merchandise of this place,
Which was spread abundantly,
Without any advertisement,
Into the bags of people's souls...

Hemlock

My heartfelt attachments,
Finally,
Have cracked...!
The clear sense of my calm desires,
These days,
Surprisingly,
Has kept me at the threshold of collapse,
And in fact,
I am always
Displeased with the fate and destiny of my time...!
It has brought things to such a point that now,
In the middle of winter,
No path is blocked by snow!
No avalanche has brought down a mountain,
And no stone has cracked from the cold...!
It has brought things to such a point that,
Even in the middle of its summer,
No spring in a secluded corner of the mountains
Flows with cool water...!
No skylark
In the meadow,
Sings a tune for its own heart...!
No eyes or gazes
From the flock of horses
Know anything...!
By the way,
Maybe Mr. Fate
Has a heart full of mud,
And
No expectation from him
For the cure of hemlock...!

Legacy

I wanted to leave a fundamental change in the world,
I worked so hard
So that my legacy
Would make the world
Cheerful in the hearts of people...
But the more I advanced,
The further I was from even reaching the hem of the world...!
I realized,
It is this world
That has left its change in me,
So quietly and without fuss,
That today,
After more than fifty years,
With all my understanding, I realized
The life I spent trying to change the world
Was like waste water
Poured into the cesspit...!

Woven Into Me

I thought
I had escaped autumn,
But even at the start of spring, I realized
Autumn had woven itself into me...!
The grass in my throat
Has become a lump...!
I thought
My life,
Was a single season...!
I gathered the journey of spring
Yesterday,
And made myself
Ready to face the dregs of fate
That I couldn't digest...!

Breathe

I always thought
The world becomes more beautiful in the morning
Dreams,
Fly out of their nests
Amid the morning clouds
And doves
Decorate the morning
With another spring in life...
And I,
With a pleasant silence,
Always think
That purity
Must be injected
From the dawn of the day
Into every second of life...
But beneath the roof of my home,
The dissonant product of the world
These days,
From the early hours,
From the very start of the morning,
From the shifting of dawn to dusk,
With the oppression of the "herds"
Of the walls of life,
I feel it upon my chest – with all its heaviness!
And still, I
In my chest,
Behind the bars of the cage,
Breathe,
Caught in the onslaught of fate's wrath,
Relentlessly,
Transforming breath into phlegm!

Drops of Water

I have been taught a few words
To survive in moments of distress
Or when
The water reaches my head
With them
To stay alive…!
So I don't suffocate, and
No matter how swift the current,
With them,
I live,
They hold my hand and never let go…
But these very words,
Always
Make me think of drowning
And
Have taken away
The chance to feel the water…!

Liberation

I've just realized;
The sea
Doesn't change
At the sight of my state...!
There is no relationship
Between us…!
The sky,
The shore,
The sea…
All of them,
In my hidden poem,
Turn into words
Filled with divine, untouched feeling...
Filled with mythical softness...
In my imagination, the sea
Sits on the prayer mat spread on the shore,
Next to my worries,
And, in thoughts of a better tomorrow,
Follows its waves,
With its full face to the sky,
Praying for me…!
I've just realized,
In the realm of "love,"
This sea
Isn't our playground…
I've just realized,
My liberation
From the snare of earthly captivity
Isn't a mere fantasy...

Waiting in Ambush for Forgotten Words

There is a pleasure
In waiting in ambush for forgotten words...!
Those that have neither become prey to romantic sentences,
Nor fallen into the trap of everyday talk.
These words
Were fewer before,
But now
They can be found more often,
Words like
Consciousness, knowledge, ethics, sincerity,
Justice, and... life.
Words that, if they were not so bare,
My endurance
Would have the power to bear them.

May 2024

Farewell

For a long time, I had wished to reduce my sleep and instead of asking the countless strangers in my dreams about our fate and the lives of those who came before us, it would have been better to clear away the mystery of the moonlight and write a poem from a world that hasn't yet fallen apart...

But on the night of my 55th birthday,

Once again in a dream, I heard the sound of an accordion played by a wandering man who always came at dusk, and we never knew where he went in the morning... He always carried a piece of bread, and when he wasn't playing the accordion, he would dip it in soda and eat it—this was the extent of his joy in life...
But when he fell asleep in the alley's curve, looking at his face, you could see centuries of silence, a silence that wore him down...

That night, at the edge of my dream, he called to me twice and wanted to give me a walnut fortune as a birthday gift! Barefoot, lost, in the house where I was born, stepping onto a damp mattress in the humid morning air of the South, I entered the waking world and felt redeemed!

In my youth, when the war sirens blared through our lives, I never imagined that these terrifying sounds would bring bad luck to our future...

I didn't foresee that they would plant endless regrets in the tree of my life...

Back then, we were content with the simple patterns of birds and flowers behind old bowls, thinking that they would guide us to salvation, and that one day, we would find redemption...

In our youth,
We didn't speak of grand words or beautiful language,
We didn't talk about the repressed voices of intellectuals in our land,
We didn't even speak of curses,
What we spoke of,
Was jasmine branches, clusters of grapes, and the two or three narcissus flowers that a gypsy woman in the marketplace had seen in our fortune... That was all.
We simply wanted,
That even if all the paths in life led to dead ends, we could plant an acacia tree in the corner of the world and create a spring of fresh water, so the weight of despair wouldn't break us...

Throughout our lives, a cold wind blew through the cracks of the window into our rooms, sowing seeds of hopelessness... Sometimes, I'd say our ship was sinking, and we had to do something...

Every time the terrifying news reached us, we'd brace for an uncertain and difficult weekend...

But I,
Was always immersed in the warmth of those around me,

hoping for better days, and now, at 55, I've lived through countless seasons...

The turmoil of these years has sometimes deceived me, but also hurt me. At times, I kept the door open at night to let the scent of flowers, even from the garden, soothe my thoughts and free me from the fear and violence outside.

In this world of defeat, I can only speak of weariness and longing, even though it might not please everyone, yet when they see my calm face, they understand that despite all the inner turmoil, **I love deeply**...

For years, the scent of native cherries in July has filled me with hope for life and love, making me feel that despite the world's darkness, I could still find peace and beauty here, beneath these trees...

But this July,

When I look through the tinted windows of the world, I no longer see it as a safe place...

Even in its best corners, you must sit in mourning, reciting laments for all that's lost...

When I put together the pieces of my life's sorrow, it forms a map of a world where I no longer know which direction to go...

So, I'm determined to walk my path, to pursue love with strength,

Even though I know,

That love in this transient world has no lasting destiny. But I must keep loving, to find my poetic home...

At 55, I've learned that even in a desert, a single firefly can shine brightly,

And that light can illuminate the world.

I know... I know

That despite the thirst that never leaves,

They've taken away our longing for rain,

But I,
Droplet by droplet,
Will discover the endless sea of love.

F
×
M

www.ingramcontent.com/pod-product-compliance
Lightning Source LLC
Chambersburg PA
CBHW072047110526
44590CB00018B/3064